THE
SOVEREIGN

To Julio,
with love,
Holly Schofield

The Sovereign

Copyright © 2022 Sarah Swain

For permission requests, write to Sarah Swain's team at:

book@sarahswain.ca

Published by Trailblazer Media Inc.

Quantity sales. Special discounts are available on quantity purchases by corporations, associations, and others. Please contact the email address above.

Paperback ISBN 9798355046170

Edited by Rebecca Brunke

Book and cover designed by Doris Chung

eBook by Ellie Sipilä

Printed in North America

THE SOVEREIGN

Sarah Swain

Ashley Correia • Cassandra Torgerson • Chelsie Meyers • Courtney Hobbs •
Holly Schefold • Jeff Eichenberger • Jen Morin • Lindsey Stefan • Lise Musso •
Meaghan Penney • Rebecca Floris • Rosanna Di Fiore • Sarah Morrison •
Selena Rae

TABLE OF CONTENTS

AUTHOR BIOS

Note to the reader

This book is a memoir-style anthology. It depicts actual events in the life of the author as truthfully as their recollection permits and/or can be verified by references found in the back of this book. Occasionally, dialogue consistent with the character or nature of the person speaking has been supplemented. The names of some individuals have been changed to respect their privacy. It is important to know and understand that the perspective and experiences of each author is their own, and their perspective and experiences are not claiming to be right, but rather, to be heard.

Within this publication, COVID-19 is spelled or referred to in a number of ways. All forms are in reference to COVID-19 - Corona Virus Disease 2019.

FOREWORD

Sarah Swain

I sat by the firepit at dusk one evening. The fire was a warm and welcome contrast to the cool, brisk air around me. There was a faint smell of decay coming from the leaves that had begun to fall, subtly mocking the death of my own reality. It was fall of 2021. The federal election had freshly concluded, and the pit of my stomach felt heavy, my nervous system uneasy. I felt a mixture of disbelief, denial, and rage as I wrestled with the reality of what was coming our way here in Canada, while the world around me continued to carry on with a level of apathy that made the hair on the back of my neck stand on end. As I stared at the flames, grief and despair slowly tightened their grip on my heart, and the tears began to fall. Digitally, anyone that appeared to think like me was being wiped off the face of the internet, so the days of wondering if I was completely out of my mind were beginning to grow. The seclusion was a special kind of hell.

As someone who has written and published several books, I fully understood the importance of storytelling and its profound impact on people's lives. Add in what I felt to be an imminent need to ensure these stories were left behind to counter the popular narrative, it only seemed fitting that I thought about writing this book. The thought of an entire side of our Canadian history going untold about these times left me feeling fearful for the next generations. However, it was an idea that came in hard and fast and fizzled out slowly as the fall turned to winter and the days grew darker, both literally and figuratively. I didn't understand it at the time, but the path I was walking was purposeful, albeit painful, lonely, and often terrifying. That path is exactly what led me to the authors you are about to meet in the pages of this book, several months later, and allowed my idea to come to fruition.

I don't believe the authors who showed up to write in this book came together by accident, either. None of us knew each other before 2021, yet somehow, we all knew we needed to share our stories— together. It was a pull that none of us could deny, and so we trusted ourselves and one another to allow our stories to unfold in the ways they were each meant to. This is precisely what I love so dearly about this book. The way in which each author came to know their innate sovereignty is so different from one story to the next. For some, the path to personal freedom began in their youth, and for others, a cataclysmic experience in adulthood set their path in motion. What brings this book together so beautifully is that our stories all intersect in 2020/2021, no matter what path we started walking individually and when. There's no denying that this compilation was meant to be.

A message to the freedom fighters

I first want to thank you for supporting the Sovereign authors by purchasing this book. I know how powerful this community is and how beautifully connected we are as we fight this good fight. I am deeply grateful for the foundation of strength this community has provided and continues to provide to so many people, as we forge onward into such uncertain times. It's my hope that as you turn the pages, you are gifted with hope, strength, courage, and love as you are reminded of your own power and sovereignty, too.

I started using my voice because so many before me were courageous enough to use theirs. While I wrestled with my own understanding of the world, these voices helped strengthen me during a time when I had never felt more fractured and disconnected from my own sense of self. Finding out just how many of us there really are felt like rocket fuel in my own healing journey. So I thank our beloved truckers and all those who took part in Freedom Convoy 2022. You came from all across Canada, representing diverse cultures, all ages and walks of life. I don't believe there is a greater force than united and sovereign souls. When those dark moments come creeping in, turn to this book for a reminder that you are not alone.

Stay strong, and keep moving forward.

A message to those who hold this book with curiosity

Thank you for being open. We've been waiting for you.

A message to those who hold this book with judgment

It's possible that the stories within this book may challenge your beliefs and worldviews. We ask that at the very least, as you make your way through each author's journey, you meet these authors with respect for their own lived experiences and the decisions they courageously made along the way. Nonetheless, we thank you for supporting these authors and providing them with an opportunity to be seen and heard.

Without further ado, welcome to The Sovereign. Thank you for being here with us.

Chapter One

SOUL SUFFICIENT

Selena Rae

Every story has a beginning, middle, and end. Let me begin with the end.

The End—Fuck Elizabeth Gilbert
2018—Age 34

The days have blurred together. It could be day three or day nine. The only thing I know for sure is that my left ass cheek keeps falling asleep, and now I have a serious case of buyer's remorse.

I can't even remember why I wanted to do this ten-day silent retreat.

Maybe because I'm some kind of masochist in denial or because so many people said I could never stay quiet that long. Or maybe it's because I'm just so broken, I've convinced myself the only way to heal is to completely shut out the external world. And I mean *completely*. I'm in the middle of nowhere, I'm not allowed to speak, read, write, or listen to anything. I'm not even allowed to make eye contact or gestures to the other masochists. I have to eat my meals facing a wall, and I meditate for twelve hours a day. I am willingly depriving myself of every comfort, in the name of what?

Yet here I sit, on my meditation cushion, cursing Elizabeth Gilbert for making millions of dollars by convincing suckers like me to try their own *Eat, Pray, Love* experience. I suppose I should cut her some slack, as I'm certain I, too, will never be able to accurately illustrate just how painful it is to sit silently for days on end, with only the company of your own mind.

I muse incessantly on this one thought: How can one person spend the majority of their life simultaneously feeling too much AND not enough? I silently scream, *I just want to be enough!* Then I feel this thought rise up, which is mine but somehow not, *Selena, you are enough.* I'm annoyed at this whimsical notion interrupting my self-beration. It continues, *You have always been enough.* I roll my eyes, but this persistent thought is enough to make me stop and remember, I chose this meditation pillow to find out who I am, to realign with myself, to build self-connection. So I sink into that knowing . . .

It brings the story of Michelangelo to mind, and I feel the tingling goosebumps that I'm starting to recognize as my confirmation sensation, rise up from my belly. I have no recollection of where I first heard this story, and although it has been deemed a tall tale, the essence of it still resonates and thus begins my journey of Soul Sufficient.

Five hundred years ago, Michelangelo was commissioned to carve the statue of David out of a large, weather-damaged slab of marble. After he had completed his task, those in awe of his work asked how he created such a masterpiece, and he simply replied, "I just removed that which wasn't David."

The Beginning—The Guitar
1988—Age 4

I'm sitting on the step, watching my dad carry his guitar case to his Monte Carlo. The guitar inside might as well be an extra appendage for how attached he is to it. He kisses me quickly, his moustache tickling my face and then petitions, "You know I love you, right?" The scented remnants of his latest binge are as familiar to me as the hoarseness of his smoker's growl. I nod, "Yes, Daddy." I'll say anything to make him happy, desperate to keep him close. But despite him serenading me a hundred times with *"Forever and ever, amen,"* while his calloused, yellow stained fingers strum, I wonder if he's singing to the six-string instead of me.

He gets in the car as he has done many times before, his guitar riding shotgun. But this time, he never comes home.

The Middle—Four, Two, and Brand New
2015—Age 31

The baby on my hip is at that exact stage where she's difficult to carry and remain productive, yet not independent enough to put down to be entertained in the Tupperware cupboard. The toddler boy, with

THANK YOU

for your purchase

Please enjoy your your first month **on me** when you subscribe to Nourish Cooking Co's Online Cooking School for Children.

www.nourishcookingcompany.com

USE CODE: "SOVEREIGN"

NOURISH
COOKING CO.

his dimples and raspy voice, is busy bulldozing his way through my legs, making my kitchen feel half its size. The preschooler, desperately vying for my attention, holds up a drawing and insists, "Mom! Mommy! Mama! Look!" It's a drawing of our family of five and a dog we don't have. I look up as I hear my husband's footsteps walking down the stairs, clearly tired after our late-night block party. The tension between us is so palpable, I wonder if anyone else can feel my blood pressure rise.

I can't tolerate his sluggish shuffle as I try to get the kids ready for church, and I lash out, anything to expel the rising discomfort. I demand an answer to a question I immediately forget asking once the words *"I'm moving out"* float from his mouth to my ears. I am caught off guard, I don't understand. The kids are loud but my heartbeat pounds so hard inside my head that it muffles the chaos in the kitchen. The world spins around me, and I reel back in time to the smell of cigarettes and the sweat of a hangover. This can't be happening. The sound of crying, which somehow isn't mine, brings me back. "I have to nurse the baby," I say as I walk past him, just so I don't have to watch him drive away, too.

The End—Naked on a Beach
2019—Age 35

Another heartbreak. Goddammit.

How can I be on this beautiful path of rediscovering my innate value, yet be constantly bombarded with men who make me feel like I'm not good enough? Another contribution to the suitcase I carry, full of evidence that tells me I am not worth the effort to love. That my heart is not meant to be a home, as disposable as the forgotten hoodie in my closet and as replaceable as his abandoned toothbrush.

Then that bubbling up sensation, not quite a voice but more of a knowing, sings to me. *If you want proof that you are worth the effort to know and love, be the proof, Selena.*

So here I am, on another quest thousands of kilometres from home, looking for evidence of my worth. I let the road take me where it will and find myself at a nude beach. I believe I'm here for a reason, so I sit down on a blanket surrounded by elderly men and women with zero fucks to give and petite college students with bodies made for nude beaches. I don't fit into either group but certainly not the latter with my body, whose beauty is likely seen in the eye of few beholders. I know the stripes, dimples, and scars are a testament to the humans my body brought into the world, but they still scream for cover.

I undress.

I don't know how to swim, but the roaring waves are calling me. I desperately text every one of my girlfriends from the blanket I cower on, "Tell me I can do this. Tell me I am brave, beautiful, and capable of walking my naked ass to the ocean so I can just love myself already!"

Radio silence. *Son of a bitch!* Tears of frustration and fear sting the corners of my eyes. I hate that knowing sensation that rises, telling me I have to do this without a cheering squad, but I listen. Tentatively, I walk my translucent bare skin suit past the pockets of people and into the ocean.

I lean back and let the ocean hold me, the chill of the water perfectly balancing the heavy gaze of the sun. I open my eyes as a shadow crosses my face. I'm only able to make out the silhouette of a man on a paddleboard. As he passes, I become acutely aware that all he can see of me are knees, nose, tits, and toes. I laugh out loud and I'm surprised to find how salty the water tastes as I choke on my embarrassment. Internally I flush, but the cool water quickly soothes the heat of humiliation and I find myself enjoying the moment. I savour the refreshing feeling of finally finding home in my own skin.

The Beginning—Long Brown Hair
1996—Age 12

I'm pretty sure I don't belong in this skin, so I spend as much time as I can numbing it so I don't feel anything at all. Stealing my mom's cigarettes, carving the initials of my crush into my flesh, or my newest release of refusing to eat, and purging when I do. I also decide to cut off all my hair because if I don't recognize myself, why should anyone else?

I walk to school in a haze, wondering if anyone will even notice. As I pass the elementary school crosswalk patrols, I catch a glimpse of one girl with long, dark hair, like mine used to be. The flash of her face hits me like ice water, and I search my mind for a clue as to why I recognize her. Another memory hits me, assaulting all of my senses, and I feel the blood drain from my face and my stomach twist. I want a cigarette or a blade, anything to help erase his face from my mind and the metal taste from my mouth. I am desperate to leave my body as my mind floods with memories of his hot, salty breath, his fat fingers on my shoulders, and his little brown car.

Another flash and I see her in a chair ahead of me in the children's church. The man at the front is wiping sweat off his forehead with one hand and holding a black Crayola marker in the other. He puts the handkerchief in his pocket and places a marker stained coffee filter in water, explaining that Jesus' love is like this water, washing away our blackest of sins. Sins like throwing up in his little brown car after he was nice enough to take me for a special sleepover.

I catch the girl's eye and feel the familiar thick haze that silently screams *me too*. I keep walking and promise myself, the next time my mom asks me if anyone has ever touched me, I'll tell her the truth, I'll tell her about the man at church five years ago. And if I do, maybe this girl won't need to cut off all her beautiful, long brown hair.

The Middle—Love Over Faith
2016—Age 32

He tells me I'm beautiful with a tone that also says I'm ridiculous because I don't know how to accept the obvious. He clearly doesn't know that I've never trusted a man who called me beautiful in my entire life.

Somehow though, the mutual brokenness between us; our failed marriages, absent fathers, abandonment by the church, it all bonds us. He challenges everything I believe, and I start to question everything I've been taught. I've been part of my religious community my entire life, and I don't know how to keep the people I love that remain as I leave the faith that raised me.

The more I question my conditioning, the more I feel drawn inward toward the voice that says, *I am good inside*. Not inherently bad, meant for a lifetime of overcoming my own nature, but instead, gifted with a lifetime to break through the layers of self-hatred that have accumulated from years of believing that I am a sinner, forever destined to strive toward an impossible standard of perfection. One that I am not meant to reach, but am expected to give up my life in quest of.

As I move away from my inherited belief system, I begin to see beauty everywhere. In myself, in humanity, in nature, in struggle, in choice. So that even when the relationship that was the catalyst for this awakening has ended in heartbreak, I keep the gifts of acceptance, awareness, and hope it initially offered me.

The End—Bedtime Love
2021—Age 38

Tonight, I honour my sadness at the injustice of having to share my greatest loves. It's not fair, no one holds their precious newborn baby in their arms and thinks, *I'm so excited to spend every second Christmas with my child.*

The phone rings, interrupting my pity party. I look to see my children video calling me and I feel a leap of joy mixed with relief. I answer and hear their voices arguing over who gets to talk to me first and I laugh to myself because it will take a few more days apart for me to miss breaking up their fights.

One after another, they request *Bedtime Love.*

Throughout the years as I have reconnected to my innate worth as a human, I have held true to one constant. *I am good inside.* When I embody this, I stay within my integrity, choosing what aligns with my highest self. I then began speaking affirmations into my children's hearts every night, making them repeat each back to me.

You are a good person. I am a good person.
You have a good heart. I have a good heart.
You are good inside. I am good inside.

I continue, affirming a growing list of qualities I hope for them to embody as they learn to believe in their intrinsic goodness.

You are kind. I am kind.
You are generous. I am generous.
You are loved. I am loved.
You are enough. I am enough.

I end this nightly mantra in honour of my own inner child, whose internal tapes from childhood have caused wounds I have been mending all my life. *I love you, Selena, but I sure don't like you.* I say the next affirmations as both a healing balm and a promise.

I like you so much. I like myself so much.
I love you the most. I love myself the most.

Just before our final goodnights, my littlest asks, "How come you say you love me the most, but I'm supposed to say I love myself the most?"

I grin, "Because it's my job to love you the most that a person can love another human being so that you know you are worthy of love."

She pauses for a moment to digest this and counters, "But I don't love myself the most, Mama, I love you the most."

"For now baby, and when you do love yourself the most, I will still love you the most that a person can love another human being."

The Beginning—Prescribed Addiction
1997—Age 13

The pain is unbearable and humiliating, and the hospital smells like disinfectant and death. The painkillers help, but the bleeding will just be something I have to live with. Even though the pain is awful, I welcome it as it allows me to enjoy a softness from my mother I haven't experienced in a long time. With her multiple jobs and my three younger siblings, I am not the priority. But now that the surgeon has confirmed I'm not faking, she sees me again.

It's not long before the endometriosis pain I suffer from one week out of the month increases to two weeks, then three, then every day. And it's not long before the prescriptions go from Naproxen to Tylenol 3, then Percocet, then Dilaudid. Every day.

The Middle—The Mirror
2016—Age 32

"You're an addict."

"What?! No, I'm not! These are all prescriptions."

"I love you, and you're a fucking addict."

"YOU'RE a fucking addict, you smoke pot all day, every day."

"Listen Selena, you're on sixteen pills a day. You're basically on synthetic heroin. You could just smoke pot and literally never take another pharmaceutical again."

So I do. Three months later, I am off every narcotic, benzo, anti-inflammatory, muscle relaxant, anti-depressant, anti-anxiety medication. Now I just smoke pot all day, every day.

I feel like a new person. Not quite back to the girl who never met a doctor with a prescription pad as a solution. But she's in there somewhere and I'm going to find her and love the shit out of her.

The End—Sovereign
2020—Age 36

Another heartbreak. For fuck's sake. What am I doing wrong?

It's time.

I'm afraid.

First the cutting, then the purging, painkillers, and now the cannabis. It all numbs the pain. Not just the physical, but the emotional pain. The pain from every kind of abandonment I've experienced, the pain from years of abuse; physical, emotional, spiritual, mental, sexual, and self-induced, the pain from never being good enough to make someone stay, choose me, love me.

It's time to feel it all, so I can heal it all.

And I am afraid.

But not as afraid as I am of looking into my children's faces and having to explain why I was never brave enough to live fully in this life, in this body. Not as afraid as I am of facing my children questioning why they weren't enough for me to choose them and love them. Not as afraid as I am of never experiencing everything this life has to offer me.

So I choose sober. I choose to feel my pain so that I may also feel joy.

I do not, however, choose the best timing. I'm two weeks fully sober and just to make things interesting, the Universe delivers a worldwide pandemic that tests my commitment to honouring my inner knowing with every government announcement, let alone my resolve to stay sober and feel everything.

I guess I also choose proving I can do hard things, again.

It is surreal, watching the world flip, offering to trade their inner knowing for an expert opinion. I have been here before; I sit back and find my centre so I don't leave my body as the flashbacks start. The father who knows best, telling his daughter he loves her as he slips away, leaving her with nothing but a sweet chorus of lies. The children's church leader who exploits the trust and faith of a little girl he preached forgiveness to, as he coerces her consent with Slurpees and slumber parties. The doctors who cash in on the trust obtained by their oath and give a teenage girl her first hit for free, while denying the human being underneath the diagnosis.

Every single memory highlights the years of dissociation, from my body and my inner wisdom, just trying to survive the manipulation of those I trusted. I thrive inside my skin now, and so when those in elected authority begin to call for me to disconnect from my body, from my knowing, *for the greater good,* I ground. When the health officials claim pharmaceuticals are *safe and effective,* and my nervous system senses the omission, I remind myself I can trust my gut. When a political governing body asks me to abandon my autonomy for the *privilege* of maintaining my human rights, I root down into my sovereignty.

And then I call that shit out, I speak my truth, I feel it all out loud. Fully fucking sober.

Conclusion—The Last Trip
2021—Age 38

I've done countless solo trips, and I've shed countless layers each time. Now here I am somewhere by the Rocky Mountains, with three complete strangers and a dog who likes me more than I like her. There's another meditation pillow and the invitation to be silent, however, I choose neither. Instead, I want to get to know the people who will be the witnesses to my spiritual journey, in more ways than I know at the moment.

On day two, the male facilitator offers me tea with floaties. I've never taken mushrooms before, despite my affinity for prescription drugs. I accept his offer of the proverbial red pill and drink the tea while I repeat my intention, *follow where the medicine leads.*

Well, what a fucking mistake that intention was.

But now I can't go back. I've fallen down the rabbit hole and the only way out is through. I'm encouraged to lay still and let the medicine take me. But I can't stay still, I can't breathe when I lay down, and worst of all, I can't shut up. *Why do I have to say every thought out loud? Oh my god, I am even saying THIS out loud! Why can't I shut up?!*

For the next six hours, the medicine brings all my secrets to the surface, which I reveal aloud to these strangers. *I hate them. I hate them for knowing. Knowing they would have a front seat to my destruction, here on my knees, screaming profanity, crying till my eyes burn. Fucking sadists with their condescending smiles. Oh my God! Why can't I stop saying everything out loud? Just shut up already, Selena.*

One horrifying moment after another, I face my demons, every last one of them.
I act like I accept my body, but I am a fraud.
I am a terrible mother and my children will want to be nothing like me.
My husband left me because I made him want to kill himself.
Hearing myself admit the last one aloud takes me out.

I'm surprised to find myself lying down now, wrapped up with the dog holding vigil at my side, and I can breathe. I'm still babbling out loud, but softly now.
I'm allowed to protect myself.
I'm allowed to take care of myself.
I'm allowed to rest.
Every terrible thing I've done was to feel safe,
I'm allowed to need to feel safe in the world.
I'm safe now.
I can breathe.
I'm okay.

My head is pounding and I smell guacamole, which I announce out loud. The three invite me to the table, but when the green mixture touches my tongue, I get sick. I return to the table and eat the bread instead. As the fog begins to lift, I tentatively ask, "Did that just happen? Did I really swear at you and call you sadists? Did I literally speak every thought out loud?" They laugh in a way that smoothly cuts through my shame and leaves me feeling accepted.

The youngest woman says, "Oh yes girl, that was magic, no pun intended."

The woman who feels like a mom to me now looks at me with awe which makes me self-conscious, "They should make a documentary about you."

I laugh and then apologize to the man who took the brunt of my angry outbursts, "I'm sorry for every *fuck you* I yelled at you."

He offers compassion so easily as he assures me, "The medicine always knows what you need."

Two days later, lying in my bed, I am sobbing over my journal as I recount my journey. My children will be home soon, will they recognize their mother? The medicine took me to the depths of my internal hell and I met the darkest part of me, my shadow. Every shameful piece of me I have denied, avoided, or abandoned. I brought my darkness into the light and now she demands her welcome, because she is worthy of knowing and loving. She is me. And I am so fucking proud of me.

***

A familiar vehicle pulls into the driveway and my children spill out with a thousand stories, their belongings piled in the front seat. The sight of them revealing my greatest fear, that I have recreated my wounds in them. The man in front of me, once my husband, showers our children with unreserved affection, and I marvel at our story's sequel, where love and loss lead to freedom and friendship. As he drives away, waving furiously until out of sight, the warmth of his devotion seals my wounds so they will never touch my children; there's no place for a guitar in that minivan.

Epilogue

When you look back on your life, there are always those significant moments in time that divide your life in half. Before and after. They are usually pivotal moments when the trajectory of your life dramatically changes course, for better or for worse, and life never looks the same again. If you mapped my turns in life on a sheet of paper, it would look like a messy scribble session from an emotional toddler.

I ponder the concept of personal sovereignty and wonder which pivotal moment graced me with that honour. I can't pick one and I can't fit them all. My life has been and continues to be an evolution of undoing. First, with noticing the marble layers created as protection from the elements of other's projections cast upon me and the subconscious beliefs adapted to shield my sensitive skin. Then, by acknowledging my remarkable ability to survive the tumultuous path I have journeyed thus far. Followed by the sometimes excruciating, but always labour-intensive, endeavour of chipping away at every sedimentary layer that covers the true essence of who I am, so that I might stand proud, not of who I have become, but who I have always been.

I still sometimes feel the weariness of this voyage, this chipping away the layers of protective residue which encapsulate my being. The removal of all that is not Selena. In moments of overwhelm, I cling to my deeply held belief and practice that in this and every moment, *I am enough*. This is Soul Sufficient.

This shedding process is lifelong but I find that notion oddly comforting. It reminds me that as long as I stay committed to self-discovery, inner alignment, and true connection, my sovereign story is not over. Which means, this is simply the end of the beginning.

SELENA RAE

Selena is a committed lifelong learner and teacher, always seeking life beyond her comfort zone. She is the mother of three small humans, and the owner of two businesses; *Soul Sufficient*, certified Life Coach specializing in self-connection and interpersonal relationships and *Sugar Mama Body Sugaring*.

Selena uses the knowledge and experience from her previous career as a Social Worker to reach others through storytelling. Her passion for connecting through resonance creates a safe space for honest and compassionate self-reflection which helps build the self-awareness that inspires one's personal growth. Selena's next writing project is a guidebook for Soul Sufficient living, where she walks alongside readers' journeys by sharing her own personal life experiences and practical strategies.

You can follow Selena's continual journey on Instagram @soul.sufficient

For my children, you are every reason I embarked on this journey of self-discovery and healing. You are my beautiful mirror and my constant reminder that love is always the answer. Deepest gratitude to my Mama for being the truest example of that enduring love. To the tribe of women I am lucky to call true friends, you have walked beside me, at times carrying me and always cheering me on, the joy of being witnessed by you is immeasurable. To my huge extended family, no one does Christmas dinner like us, and I cherish each of you. To each and every individual who has been a part of my life story, whether positively or painfully, you are a welcomed part of my journey, I thank you for every ounce of love or lesson you have bestowed upon me.

"And last but not least. I wanna thank me . . ." –Snoop Dogg

In this & every moment
You are enough.

I SRae

Chapter Two

MEDICAL 'MARY'-GO-ROUND

Sarah Morrison

I see her. For the first time in six years, I can see her. She looks like the woman I knew all my life and yet, she's different. Happier. She has this beautiful long, brown hair and she's surrounded by a golden hue. I think the most striking thing about her is her presence. She radiates love and peace. I feel lighter. I start getting these images, almost as if she wants me to see them. Dad is having lunch at work, my brother in his dungeon, which she used to call our basement, and my older brother on a job site. But what calms me the most are the images I'm seeing of my children. My babies that never knew her love, her laughter, her kisses. Suddenly, I am seeing them as she sees them, in all their childhood innocence, and now I know they are never without her. Just as I am relishing this reunion, I'm brought back to my breath. As my breathing returns to normal, she fades again like the memories I have of her. Slowly fading as the years pass. Suddenly, I'm awake.

For years, I have been longing to see her in my dreams. I search for signs of her every day and try to imagine she is at peace. My last memories of her are tainted with trauma, but thanks to a dear friend who journeyed with me through my first shamanic breathwork session, I had my first glimpse of a peace I never knew existed. An existence for her that is free from the suffering she endured for many years with a rare illness. I have lived with the trauma of my mother's illness and more profoundly, her death, since she departed on the first day of spring 2016. I was unaware at the time but as my mother's soul departed, I was being reborn. As the world was waking up once again to longer days, warmer sun, and the growth of spring blossoms, I was ushering in a new energy of spirit, a conscious awakening.

What I remember of my childhood was a lot of "I can't" or "we can't." A life of limitation due to crippling pain, discomfort, and anxiety. Perhaps my fondness for summer and warm weather has to do with the fact that it holds my happiest memories. Memories of days spent with family at the beach, cottages, camping in our trailer, splashing around in the pool. Summer was always full of laughter and Coppertone. On the flip side, winters were dark and brought out the worst of her condition. I remember many colds and flus that lingered, sores that never healed, and nights I would find her crying alone in her room. My mother's strength was truly admirable, but she was always her most vulnerable with her family.

I stumbled on her old medical records and found an article she must have turned to, to help her understand the early days of her illness, titled "Turning to Stone." Pre-diagnosis, my mom was quite literally turning to stone. If you're a fan of the late Bob Saget, you'll know the prominent role he played in the Scleroderma Research Foundation. My whole life, whenever I shared with someone that my mother had Scleroderma, I was met with bewildered faces. Few people know about the disease, even less so when she was diagnosed twenty-eight years ago, so when my parents found a competent specialist in Toronto, there was hope for a treatment plan. It was a treatment plan that required close monitoring as she was taking some very harmful drugs. This is where her dependency on medication began.

A couple of decades later, we found ourselves in a heartbreaking situation, one that would change our family forever. It was a cold, dark day in January, sitting with my mom in the ICU, waiting on the doctors that would deliver her fate. My dad and I were there when they came to tell us that it was an incurable glioblastoma. A brain tumour. I had more strength than I give myself credit for, but the only thing I could do in that moment was drop to my knees. I sobbed until I felt nauseous, crippled by the thought of my future without her. Then I picked myself up and resolved to do the best I could to support her until the bitter end. This moment is forever etched in my memory as one that sparked a lifelong journey of questioning. So many questions. Why was my mother a target of so much suffering? Why did it have to end this way? What could we have done differently for her? This last question is the one that still haunts me. I have learned so much about what it means to be healthy and how we can best support our bodies through nutrition and natural modalities. I feel anger that I didn't do the work earlier in life, that I dutifully listened to all medical advice and followed it to a tee when it came to easing her symptoms. A prescription for this, a cream for that. A pill to help with this symptom that was caused by that medication. I realize now what a dizzying dance it was, keeping all the medications and side effects in check all those years. As I sit here writing these pages, the anger bubbles up again. I was young when mom got sick, but as I got older, I could have asked more questions. I could have helped her to do her due diligence when it came to her medications. I could have taken the initiative to help cook healthier meals. I could have . . .

Releasing this guilt is a work in progress, but what it boils down to is dependence. Dependence on a system that only contributed to the cyclical nature of pharmaceuticals and side effects. I knew in my gut that it was this dependence that ultimately led to her brain tumour. She was on a heavy-duty toxic cocktail of pharmaceuticals for her disease, and aside from some physiotherapy in the early days, there was zero emphasis on other forms of treatment, like homeopathy for some of the more mild nuisances like sleep. I am ashamed to admit that it was not even her death that initially woke me from my medicalized haze, but rather my desire to start a family. I thought back to my own youth and realized that I, myself, had become dependent on the same system that failed my mother. Chronic fatigue treated with antidepressants? No need to question the logic there (insert sarcastic tone). I have one of the same positive markers my mom had when she was diagnosed, so I am monitored twice a year by a rheumatologist, should I develop the same disease. What is unknown to me is whether or not the disease is genetic. I may not be able to control my genetics, but I resolved to control my environment, not only for myself but for the future I wanted for my children.

Prior to getting pregnant with my firstborn, I put in the necessary work to distance myself from the sick care system. I started to read the labels in the grocery stores, I researched the potential chemicals in our home and threw out all the scented soaps, candles, and perfumes. I immediately went off contraceptive medication after doing a deep dive into the harms courtesy of Dr. Kelly Brogan. All of these felt like such simple fixes to a much larger issue. We are not set up to support ourselves properly, and we lack confidence in our own functioning immune systems. We also live in a very toxic world and have come to view this as normal. The next few generations of children are growing up sicker than the ones before them, and we have to wonder why?

When I got pregnant with my daughter, instinct kicked in and I felt so protective of all the choices I was making that would impact her. I did not want her walking the same bumpy road I had walked and experience the loss of a mother so early in life. I was twenty-nine when my mom died, and while I was newly married and living in our first home, I had yet to experience so many of the joys that life has to offer with her by my side. This would not be my daughter's experience. I made a promise to her when she was born that I would fight like hell to live longer. I am now a year older than my mom was when she was first diagnosed, so I must be doing something right. I began my pregnancy journey by doing my own research on all the recommendations that are given to you by the so-called experts. I know what you're thinking, and no, I didn't just Google opinions, I put in the hard research. The long hours reading studies and journals, the history of disease, and the importance of nutrition. My partner and I have made a lot of choices for our kids that stem from a toxic dependence on the medical system. We hope to raise them to have faith that their bodies are miraculous things that can be supported through illness with the right tools. We do not want them to fear viruses and bacteria, but rather welcome them as an upgrade for their bodies and their immune systems. If you see where I am going with this, you'll notice the natural segway into Covid-19.

Now, because of my natural affinity to question everything, I very quickly began to see the holes forming in the mainstream narrative surrounding the best ways to keep us safe. Like everyone else, we put in our "two weeks to flatten the curve." We explored the great outdoors, we baked, we danced, and we spent amazing quality time as a family of three. Once the two weeks were over with no signs of slowing down, I did what I always do. I researched for myself.

Thinking back to that harrowing time in 2016, there is a moment in my mom's brain cancer journey that still haunts me. She was two weeks post-op from her emergency brain surgery and we had managed to get her transferred from Toronto Western, where they did her first surgery and gave us her diagnosis, back to Royal Victoria Hospital. It was there that the doctors did some scans when her pain worsened and realized she was experiencing significant swelling in her brain. She would need to go under the knife again. She was transferred back to the emergency department at Toronto Western, where she spent over twenty-four hours waiting for another surgery. I had arrived at the hospital in the evening to relieve my dad, who would make his way home to get some sleep. In the span of a few short hours, mom took a turn for the worse. This is such a raw moment to share because I never talk about it with anyone, but it still gives me nightmares. As a child, no matter how old you get, you will always see your mom as your protector. She is the strong woman that birthed you, calmed you when you cried, kissed away all the boo-boos, healed your broken hearts with her hugs, and shared the wisdom only years spent raising children could offer. To see your mom the way I saw her that night, so fragile and knocking on death's door, that does something to a person. It's the thought that in the blink of an eye, all the safety you knew growing up would be gone. Around 8:00 pm that night, mom couldn't swallow her medication. She became too sleepy, or so the nurse told me, but I had a hunch it was worse than that. She had also been sick to her stomach, so the nurse pumped her with anti-nausea medication to hopefully offer her the opportunity to rest. Around 2:00 am, mom began vomiting bright, red blood. Things moved quickly after that, but I remember running into a deserted ER hallway screaming, "HELP!" Then I was a child again, standing there desperate for someone to save my mother, feeling helpless and alone. The neurologist came down, asking mom to perform simple commands, which she of course could not. Her pupil had also blown, so they got her started on a saline drip and intubated her. I remember the doctor saying this bought them an extra half hour to an hour of time. We were so close to losing her that night, and I reverted to a scared little child. I huddled in a dark waiting room alone and cried. I didn't want to see her like that. I was imagining these would be my last memories of her, and it only made me yearn more for the mother I once knew.

The woman who loved to brush my hair, who could make me laugh with her sarcasm and her jokes, whose own laugh was so contagious you'd want to wrap yourself up in it. I only started to breathe again once they took her in for surgery and my dad arrived. This moment is the moment that paralyzes me when I think back to it. It's also the moment that centres around all the decisions I make in my life. I think of my own fragile children and how I never want them to experience what I experienced.

When the covid vaccine became readily available, I had multiple reasons to pause and really think about it. For starters, I was pregnant with my third baby, and there were no safety studies done to properly assure pregnant women as much as they like to say there were. I had a very traumatic septic miscarriage with my second pregnancy, so I was dealing with the anxiety of that, and I was being extra cautious with the choices I was making. I think the biggest one for me was seeing the very real adverse reactions that were happening to real people. I was seeing women with very severe neurological reactions resembling seizures, and I was transported right back to that ER room with my mom. The risks for me did not outweigh the benefits, and I refused to see my children become collateral damage just so I could appease others. When you've laid with your mother, the woman that brought you into this world, and witnessed her take her last breath, not much else can frighten you. I don't fear a virus that ended up giving me mild cold symptoms, I fear for a future where my children watch me suffer with a debilitating condition. I want them to have the childhood I never had with a mother who can do ALL the things. I want to get down in the snow and build forts. I want to travel the world and have adventures with them. I want to play sports and run around wild and free with them, and I want to continue to carry them until they decide they are big enough to journey on their own.

I think what's important to know is that we are all capable of making smart, rational decisions for ourselves. We often lack the courage to seek out the hard truths because we tell ourselves that we aren't smart enough, aren't equipped to analyze data or trained to know how to handle the big things like our own medical decisions.

We also feel so overwhelmed by the hustle and bustle of life that we rationalize it by saying we lack the time. We rely on the experts because they were the ones that put in the long hours, the many years of schooling, so we didn't have to. Right? Wrong! No one is as educated on your own family history and your own body, as you are! I decided after my mom's death to stop handing over my power to others in the hopes that they can make everything go away. We outsource our health because it's easier. When I have a migraine, is it easier for me to pop an Advil than to get to the root of it or to try other remedies? Of course, it is! Fast medicine is easy medicine, but it doesn't mean it's what's best for our bodies. Sleep, nutrition, vitamins, social connection, are all things that take real commitment and real energy to prioritize. We all know that there are a myriad of ways to treat ailments that don't have us relying on medications that always come with side effects. Western medicine can be a lifesaver in times of emergency, but as a preventative, it is set up to create lifelong subscribers.

My decision to opt out of the Covid-19 vaccine should not be a controversial one. It should not be the reason I am barred from participating in everyday life, in travel. Especially now that we know it does nothing to prevent transmission. My personal health decisions are being laid bare for all to see because we have a government that prefers to demonize rather than respect personal choice. As a woman in my third pregnancy and then breastfeeding, and as someone who also read the nine pages of adverse reactions only to see the very illness that plagued my mother for over twenty years, I made an educated decision based on the available research. I am saddened to see what has become of our beloved country and the people in it. My inner child is scarred from years of medical trauma with my mother, and now I live in a country that wants to coerce people into putting themselves at risk just to enjoy basic freedoms. I stand firm in my choice, and I will continue to fight for others to have that same choice.

As Maya Angelou once wrote, "a wise woman wishes to be no one's enemy; a wise woman refuses to be anyone's victim." I refuse to be a victim of a failed system only to see my children as the ones that truly suffer.

SARAH MORRISON

Sarah Morrison lives in Hamilton, ON, with her husband and two children. She followed her passion for teaching to North Bay and received her Bachelor of Education from Nipissing University. Sarah worked in various schools across Simcoe Muskoka and Halton regions prior to helping establish a new alternative schooling model. When she's not working, Sarah loves to spend time with her family. She also has a passion for travel and exploring all this beautiful world has to offer. Her mother, Mary, is the inspiration behind her story, and Sarah continues to honour her mother's legacy by sharing her heart with others. Sarah's goal is to inspire children (including her own) to be steadfast in their beliefs and fearless in their pursuit of happiness.

To my children, Olivia and Noah, may you always know the strength that comes from speaking from your heart and staying true to yourself. May you forge ahead, leaving the trauma of the past behind you as you find your true, authentic selves. I love you both to the moon and back.

I want to thank my dear husband, Alex, for always believing in me and encouraging me to live life on my terms. You are the greatest partner to ride the highs and lows of life with.

To my Pops, thank you for allowing me to share our story and for always letting me spread my wings. We endured the most trying of times together as a family, and now we have a beautiful angel to walk with us through the rest of our days.

Through all the grief and trauma
you've endured, I hope you find
the confidence to always live
your truth ♥
   much love to you,
      Sarah Morrison

Chapter Three

FLIGHT OR FIGHT

Jen Morin

2020 was a year to remember for all of us, obviously. My whole world began to collapse for a slew of reasons. It was an inevitable fall from an unstable foundation, triggered by a traumatic heartbreak, isolation, and the slow destruction of any outside world safety and comfort that I once knew.

The pattern of our society is to cover our pain and discomfort with drugs, alcohol, another relationship, anything to avoid looking within ourselves, but I found myself in a position where I couldn't seem to cover the pain I was feeling. I couldn't watch TV at all. My previous interests or void fillers simply weren't working. I couldn't focus on anything and was barely hanging on. I was down to these two options: I either take myself out of this world and misery, or I keep learning and digging to find a way out.

The rules and regulations being forced upon us didn't feel right to me. It was a deep sense of knowing that no matter what, separating people from each other is about the worst thing you could do. Day and night, I was alone in my house. Suddenly there was nowhere to go, no one to see. This sort of shock to my previously ingrained pattern of go, go, go in life, was an explosion to my stability. I had just lost a man I hoped for a future with, and I wasn't allowed to see the friends, family, and coworkers I knew and loved. Some dreams were put on hold, and some were blown up entirely. Without love and connection, it all seemed so pointless. It felt like I fell into a black hole or, more accurately, an alternate fucked up universe.

I already held a good base of mental health practices and knowledge because of dealing with anxiety and depression from a rough start in life, but nothing could keep me stable for more than a few minutes without strenuous effort. Every step forward I made internally, something new and illogical would appear in the outside world. The different rules for sitting and standing, certain activities restricted after a certain time, the cloth of any material masks, the arrows on the floor as if passing someone from a particular direction mattered. Small businesses being forced to close, but large ones allowed to be open. The inconsistencies between the rules kids were following at school, and the way people were having to test and isolate in the workplace. The particular stats that were and weren't being shown, and lack of looking at existing health, lifestyle, and diets of people who were getting sick. And importantly, the absolute disregard for the mental impact being caused by lockdowns and confusion, with me fully knowing that mental health plays a massive role in overall mortality.

Survival mode had kicked in full swing, and I couldn't stop researching, studying, and learning every waking second. I found myself making a binder of facts, stats, studies, and articles. My entire world had become a raging fire, and I was determined to understand why what was happening in the world just didn't feel right to me. The days went by slowly. There was not much difference between any particular day or time. Nothing to look forward to, no future plans, and absolutely filled with fear from what I was starting to see. It was the most bizarre world. Trying to work at home all alone, staring into space, trying to sort the confusion in my mind and heart.

The polarity of what I could see outside and what I believed I knew inside, was crippling me with what felt like encroaching insanity. It was either I had gone mad, or the world had, so I kept digging to find out which statement appeared to be more true. The first question on the table was, "why do I believe what I believe?"

*　*　*

I had always been into natural health and natural remedies. Growing up as a kid, my stepmom kept us in check on not consuming too much sugar or processed goods. As I grew older and experienced some health hiccups, I became more cautious and made continual changes toward becoming healthier and more natural in any way possible. When my personal experiences with our healthcare system and the veterinary system proved failure time and again, I became my own doctor for my four-legged friend and I. People can judge all they want, but my personal experience with a more eastern medicine approach, and range of natural practices, was a success every time. The more I learned, I became less and less dependent on the medical and veterinary systems and fell more in love with nature and the magic of this planet. Adapting natural health principles and knowledge absolutely became part of who I am and my daily life, and my health reflects real results.

Suddenly, I found myself in a world where this whole concept of being naturally healthy was being judged, shamed, and outright expelled as though it wasn't even an option. I couldn't believe we were starting to go down this path of literally eradicating the idea of proactively being a naturally healthy human. There were many avenues of the pandemic that could be evaluated more closely to easily reveal that things didn't line up with being good for us as a whole. But most people weren't paying attention and were simply doing what they were told. It was a continuous struggle for me to balance those wishing for the death of people like me, and the desire to hold on to what I knew and believed.

One by one, more and more things I loved were taken away, and finally, the career I enjoyed and was good at arrived on the chopping block. Having to hand my bodily autonomy and health over to someone else felt like rape. It felt like despair. It felt like I did not want to fucking participate. Especially knowing full well that getting my own shot did nothing for anyone else's health, despite the intense marketing campaign that stated otherwise. I *knew* and understood this part of the science with all my being. Yet still, I was being treated like I was leaking disease. My employer, who likes to pride themselves on being champions of mental health, was making me take courses on inclusion, ethics, and diversity, while at the same time telling myself and others that our beliefs, knowledge, culture, and religions did not matter. Basically, telling me that the large part of who I am, and all I know about *my* health, and natural health, needed to be ignored without question. The hypocrisy was eating me alive.

I knew that if you don't have health, you literally have nothing. My childhood pushed me to be completely (*overly, if I'm being honest*) independent. My ability to look after myself was absolutely integral to getting what I wanted and needed in life. I felt like I had three options. One: bend over, accept soul death, take the shot, hope to God I don't have major side effects, *and* hope it's not an ongoing requirement. Two: run and hide in the woods. Or three: fight for nature, for humanity, and for what feels right deep within my soul. However, there really was no choice to be made. Every bit of me knew option one wasn't happening. Option two wasn't really possible logistically, and not ideal without a man to join me. So option three it was. I kept following my intuition and my naturally ingrained personality to fight.

Ironically, my first unpaid day was Remembrance Day. The freedoms our ancestors fought for were forever changed in my mind. My employer offered no severance, and the government would not provide EI. There was no care, compassion or empathy for those of us who felt differently, or how we would be able to provide food and shelter for ourselves going forward, let alone the impact this would have on our mental, emotional, and spiritual health.

If I thought I was unstable before with my crazy person's binder of facts, it paled in comparison to where I found myself after losing my job. My mind was racing and I was in a chronic state of unrest, suffering through the worst state of anxiety imaginable. I pictured my mind as specks of energy, of thoughts, floating aimlessly in space. I couldn't eat. I wasn't looking after my home or myself. I couldn't stop crying. An endless loop of questions played in my mind. *How was I going to pay the bills? Am I going to lose my home? How could*

I even attempt to work anywhere else in this mind state? My writing was scattered, riddled with anger. Terrified for any future I could possibly see. Random scribbles. *"This is fucked! Please wake up!"* I was continually trying to convince myself that things could change, things will get better. Repeating over and over, *"There's no way this is actually happening."* I didn't know what to do, and also knew that no one could help me. No counsellor, no parent or friend, no manager. This was bigger than them. One of the largest corporations and our own prime minister were in on this destruction.

I knew my mind state was scary. I couldn't stop. For a while, the more I learned about the world, the worse it got, but at the same time, the more I learned, the more I knew I was on the right path. Where could I go? How could I escape? I couldn't handle the manipulative behaviour and gaslighting that was being executed by our government in power. They were promoting fear and division! They were creating a disaster, and I could see what it was doing to everyone's mental health.

Doctors, psychologists, scientists, and lawyers were being censored on things they had studied their whole lives. People were getting shamed and discriminated against for speaking anything that didn't match the narrative the media was preaching. No discussion was allowed. Regular citizens who considered themselves to be "good people" were convinced to hate others because of their own fear. Compassion seemed to dissolve into thin air. "No hate here" signs started to cause me trauma because it was impossible to ignore the hate I was feeling from friends, family, and strangers. I wanted out of the world I could see. Between being scared of being put into a camp for the intolerable unvaccinated, not having the authority to choose what I put into my body, and the fear of the world spiralling into apocalyptic chaos while not having a man by my side, I was in a constant state of terror. All of the pain, combined with the isolation and confusion, was creating the perfect storm and leading me down an unexpected journey.

I knew there had to be a way to combat what I was feeling without drugs. I could not handle the ridiculousness of having to take a pharmaceutical to calm the mind state that was triggered by not wanting to take a pharmaceutical. And so, I chose to be with the pain and allow it to guide me to where I needed to go. It led me to mental health principles, to psychology and the subconscious mind, to philosophy, to the collective consciousness, to religions, further into nature and patterns of nature, to quantum physics, energy, to individuality and sovereignty, to being able to hold love for even those who hurt us. Things finally started to come together towards peace.

I started listening to other people's stories online, looking for hope. Hearing from nurses, doctors, pilots, and police, helped me to feel less alone, as these were clearly good and intelligent people who shared similar beliefs. I started following philosophers and psychology experts to learn to sort out the confusion and chaos in my mind. I started following spiritual teachers and mentors to unfold the pain I was feeling in my heart. I became so grateful for these people, their knowledge, and the ability to listen to wisdom from even those dead and gone.

Gratitude became a big focus in general, remembering that I was receiving endless lessons on mistakes I felt I made in love and in my life. I rooted myself in knowing that what I was learning would benefit me and others in the future. I reminded myself that I did have beautiful humans in my life who were understanding of where I was at and who cared for my well-being. The community online who were in the same boat as me brought daily relief. Despite the way the media tried to paint the picture, everyone in the health freedom and sovereignty movement across the world was sharing endless knowledge and truly desired and embodied love and unity for all. My gratitude for the internet and technology went to a whole new level. Funny enough, building "the internet" was part of that career I lost.

Nature became key to daily grounding. My feisty senior puppy basically dragged me out of the house on the days I didn't want to move. She knew what was best. Nature was what made me hang on, between this magical animal I got to hang out with each day and the feeling of relief when I was amongst trees, rivers, and endless natural beauty. Slowly the momentum of feeling better started to build. The isolation forced me to keep looking within since there was nothing I could do to change the outside world.

Understanding the laws of manifestation, I started to examine how I'd arrived in this space in my life. I laid all my cards on the table and took a good look at the mess I was left with, both mentally and physically, after all my stability burned down. Physically, I was able to see that one of my patterns for covering discomfort in the past was shopping. I had accumulated so much stuff from always chasing the high I got from good deals at auctions and yard sales. The ridiculous amount of things I had but didn't need was in my face each day, reminding me of what needed to be cleaned and decluttered, both literally and figuratively, in my life. Each time I would crash again, this would become my grounding focus. *"Get my house cleared out,"* because even if I was running off to the woods, this needed to be done. I think it's Jordan Peterson who I learned the theory from, that when you don't know where to go or what to do, the very first thing to do is to clean up your room or your house. My willpower to feel better, and not seeing any other way to move forward in that moment, was the continual emotional guidance. This forced focus made clear progress, even if it was baby steps.

I was starting to realize how focused we all are on the material world, always aiming for more and more, always trying to get somewhere, find someone, make a certain amount of money, and *then* we will feel good. I realized I was taking everything so seriously and not holding enough gratitude for the endless beautiful people, things, and experiences I already had in my life. I would never again take any human interaction for granted, and be sure to appreciate their jokes, their help, sharing their gifts, knowledge, love, and time.

I was forced to surrender to the unknown of the future. Learning about energy taught me that everything is constantly moving and changing. Nothing's ever certain, and anything is possible. It was extremely challenging to let go but became a welcome relief. I started to be able to detach myself from heavy-weighted desires and outcomes I previously had for my future, many of which had been formed unconsciously, simply to cover the pain. I had been running very passionately but aimlessly for so long.

As time went by, I realized I had actually manifested this time alone. For my whole life, I was never able to have the opportunity to wake up and decide what to do with my time. I always felt strapped by things to do, places to go, and expectations to live up to. This forced me to slow right down and regroup. Finally, I got to and *had to* choose. The isolation forced me to become creative with what I had in front of me. It gave me the opportunity to discover who I truly am and what I actually want to spend my time and energy on. I had the time to notice where I was not respecting myself or others, and could actually do better. It was a process of separating all of the stories and patterns I either consciously or unconsciously fell into. It was realizing it is okay to feel different and be a little weird. Trying to be less weird would mean trying to be less of who I am. It was finally making a conscious effort to stop doing things I don't want to do, and learning to trust myself, forgive myself, and follow what feels right for me. I was in full belief that we are all equal and deserve the right to our own path and individuality. The desire to have my free will respected also helped me to understand the importance of free will for all.

Being out in public amongst others who were living like nothing was wrong was a special kind of pain, but I realized it was my pain and not theirs. I could see that I was in a position no different than some humans in this world who may be suffering from not having food, shelter, or clean water, and them feeling like all of the other humans who aren't affected go about their daily life and simply don't care. This was all proof that even darkness has its purpose. This pain and grief were bringing invaluable lessons. Polarity in the human experience truly is necessary for positive evolution.

The pieces of the mess in the outside world finally started coming together, too. It seemed like either a lot of people in powerful positions are absolutely detached from themselves and compassion for others' realities and experiences, or is it that they actually don't want us to be strong? And they don't want us to be all united and filled with love? If we are, then we wouldn't be able to be controlled for their gain and the execution of their desires, as we would be focused on our own. I knew the pattern of suppressing knowledge, censorship, and burning books has existed for as far back as you can research, but my heart could see that, in general, the masses are trying to do their best in their jobs and in their lives. We are all here to create. Not to give our creative power away to others and to systems that don't align with our talents, our values, and our worth. When things *feel* right and we feel good, we have more energy to help others. It seemed so simple to me, but many are blocked and confused by their own pain and fear and just end up just following the herd out of comfort and ease.

When we lose our connection to nature, we forget that we are part of nature and that we need nature to survive. We forget that we are all one connected system, which is made up of fractals of our individual selves, where each and every decision we make has an effect on both our inner and outer worlds. Scientists from Dr. Elmer Green to Aristotle have known the connection between mental state and physical health. It has become so clear that the health and safety of the world really boils down to the individual state of our minds and is absolutely not dependent on pharmaceutical products.

We are ultimately free. We have free will and willpower. We make millions of decisions every day. Each and every one is done individually, for each person, based on a different set of information we each hold. The information we are exposed to is all we know. No one is *required* to do something else for you. We are all one, but everyone is on their own journey and holds equal worth. Once we know better, only then can we do better, so forgiveness of others and ourselves is of utmost importance.

It was my choice to continuously choose faith over fear and own my life, that led me out of the chaos and despair. It was my desire to feel better that laid the path, little by little, in each present moment. I was a Tasmanian devil of sorts. We all are. We need to process the chaos and energy that we've gathered throughout our experiences, organize it, and follow the path that feels best. The path that we choose, not that we're running from. Follow the heart. Love is organized energy. It was my ability to hold and focus on love that helped me stay in this world, no matter how uncertain and painful it felt. What we focus on is what we get. This is our reality. Decisions that feel good bring a light, high energy. Decisions that feel bad bring a heavy, dark energy. Then we carry it around. My journey was showing me how much it hurts to be pushed into someone else's box and the importance of equal worth. You deserve your choices to be yours and follow what feels good, just as much as I deserve my choice, and to follow what I know.

I discovered this world is way more magical than we realize, and we're way more connected than we know. Every human gets these downloads, this knowledge, this guidance, but you have to unload the distractions to be able to hear it clearly. Call it what you want, intuition, God, higher self, source, spirit. It is real.

This time, my intuition was so loud and clear that I was pushed to believe in myself, even when no one else did. All I had to do was survive. Keep taking one small step after another and still be able to look for the love, no matter how hard it got, and the momentum did build naturally. Survival mode and persistence have a purpose. Survival is the way "out." Keep believing and looking for the one next breadcrumb in each present moment. Trust it will be laid and built where you direct it, and so I choose to trust myself.

JEN MORIN

Jen is a natural creator and problem solver. First time author in the Sovereign, she takes you through a pivotal time in her journey of mental wellness, awakening, and her connection to nature.

Growing up in a small town, she experienced a lot of freedom as a wild 80's kid. A child of divorce, she got to experience the beauty and challenges of large split families. She was taught the importance of hard work and to pull her own weight in the family responsibilities. There was never a boring moment.

She had dozens of jobs through her teens and twenties, and finally landed a career in the corporate world, where she was able to develop her true engineering and creative mind. She discovered antiques when she was young, became addicted to the hunt for unique treasures, and has been buying and selling used goods for nearly twenty years.

Jen is a proud aunt to two nieces and six nephews between all of the siblings. Chloe, her feisty canine friend, has been the true love of her life so far, and has been along for nearly fifteen years of adventures. Always filled with energy, Jen has never sat still, spent as much time as possible outside in the sun and in nature, and has continually been striving toward her goals.

With a drastic life change after the pandemic, Jen is diving deeper into creativity and repurposing salvaged materials, sharing all she's studied on mental health, psychology, and our connection to nature with writing her own mental health workbook, and starting a company with some friends in hopes to help others align with natural health and wellness, and individual sovereignty.

The abundance of friends and family around me, my long-time counsellor, the natural universe, and my intuition.

Follow what feels best, always.

Chapter Four

MY GOLDEN (CANCELLED) TICKET TO FREEDOM

Rebecca Floris

"You need to drive to the bank and deposit this money so I can cancel these tickets."

I sputtered these words as I shoved money into Chris' hands and gave him the car keys.

We had spent the majority of the night discussing the implications of leaving Canada, where lockdowns had just ended, to going to New Zealand, where lockdowns had just started.

It seemed to both of us the idea of leaving was not wise due to the circumstances surrounding both countries. It had taken us three hours of heavy discussions the night before the flights to make the decision to cancel the flights and stay in Canada indefinitely. It also seemed silly to me that we didn't have any money in either of our bank accounts to pay for the $200 cancellation fee for the flights, but we had taken all of our cash out to exchange it in New Zealand.

"The agent says he has to process the cancellation fee before midnight, otherwise we won't get the refund for the tickets."

"Fuck! Okay, bye!" Chris ran to the car and sped off toward the nearest bank machine, which was a good twenty minutes away. Either he made it to the bank on time, or we would have to take the flights after all—a prospect which scared me and thrilled me.

I paced the room impatiently while I waited for a confirmation text from Chris to tell me he had made the deposit.

"The money is in the bank."

I hastily relayed the message to the travel agent on the phone so he could process things on his end.

"Ma'am, the cancellation fee has gone through—the flights are cancelled. You should automatically receive a refund within seven days. If you don't, call us back."

I thanked the agent, hung up the phone and called Chris.

"It's done."

"Now what?"

"I don't know . . ."

***

It took me eight months to finalize my New Zealand nursing license, obtain a job offer, apply and wait for my visa to be approved, and secure a spot in a Managed Isolation Quarantine (MIQ) facility.

After all of these things had fallen into place, I excitedly booked tickets for September 2021, looking forward to pursuing my dream of immigrating to New Zealand. When the entire country went into lockdown in August, I was devastated but hopeful the lockdowns would end before I was due to fly. I realized this was my last opportunity to leave Canada before the imposition of mandatory vaccination passports in Canada for aviation travel. If I didn't take the flights, I would lose my opportunity to go anywhere in the world for an undetermined amount of time. I would also lose my dream job and future plans.

Ever since I returned to Canada in 2020, I had wanted to leave again. I was in love with the idea of living in New Zealand. I made plans to take my nursing career there and begin a future with Chris where we would go back and forth from Canada to New Zealand, follow the eternal summer, and buy a gold claim where we would pan for gold. Before the pandemic, we had followed the Canadian/New Zealand summer for two years and had plans to elope on the Franz Josef Glacier in New Zealand. All of those plans got cancelled as a result of a private medical decision.

I felt like it was crazy to give up the opportunity to immigrate to New Zealand and work as a nurse. I wanted to go to Queenstown so badly, and I knew from the outside it looked as if I was giving up everything when I cancelled the flights, but when I cancelled the flights, I found my truth.

The truth is, I've always been a little strange. Even when I was a kid, I found myself lost in books instead of competitions. I would write in my journal and think about the things I wanted in my life. In my journals, I would set goals, make plans, and discuss them with myself, as any avid writer does. I loved reading and writing and as a child, I wanted to pursue writing as a career, but the lure of financial gains tempted me into nursing instead.

I flew through nursing school and graduated with outstanding academic achievement. I came to find working as a nurse was a totally different experience compared to being a student nurse. I can't explain the confusion and mild disgust I felt when patients told me about their experiences within the health care system. I had always assumed Canadian health care worked well. These patients were telling me otherwise. They told me intimate secrets about their illnesses, ideas, and treatments, and expected me to help them solve all of the problems they were having with a system so clearly broken. This system was reliant upon people getting and staying sick in order for the money to flow. The health care system seemed destined to fail and make everyone sick in the process. There were always more problems than there were solutions, and the symptoms of illnesses were tucked away under four or five different prescriptions instead of being addressed outright. Eventually, I decided I wanted to transition away from working within traditional health care modalities and turn toward holistic healthcare models where I could become an entrepreneur. This shift in my nursing practice was inadvertently the beginning of a series of events that landed me in New Zealand.

***

When I got off the plane for the first time in Queenstown, I was in indescribable awe. I can only explain it as falling in love. Everything was different and magical and beautiful. I would awaken in "the morning to the birdsong of the Tūī who lived in the forest." I would accompany Chris on explorations involving rivers and gold. We would take long hikes into the untouched wilderness where we slept on hard wooden frames in old, unkempt huts in the mountains where we were surrounded by the screams of the invasive Australian Possum. We would dance the evenings away at downtown bars where we drank espresso martinis and imagined ourselves to be as posh as the customers who frequented our workplace, the prestigious Matakauri Lodge. In the midst of all of these wild experiences, both

Chris and I encountered some of the most unique and wonderful people we had ever met in our lives—happy, lively, slightly alcoholic, outgoing, and incredibly generous. Every day was an adventure in Queenstown, and I treasured every moment of time I spent there, for I had never experienced anything like it. I found my truth in New Zealand and realized I would be much better suited to their climate. This was when I decided I wanted to live there forever.

***

The pursuit of eternal happiness is an unrealistic goal, but I somehow believed if I moved to New Zealand, I would be endlessly happy. I defined success as immigrating to New Zealand and working as a nurse, although I was loath to think about the logistics of the plan. It wouldn't be going too far to say I was obsessed with the idea of immigrating to New Zealand.

I know there was a reason for me to think these things, and it still pains me to remember what has happened over the last several years and how my plans have had to be rewritten. I still don't know what the future holds for me. It is hard to see a path forward at times, but I have hope. I regret cancelling the tickets, but I also wouldn't go back and change any of the experiences I have been through as a result of that decision, including the postponement of my dream life. When all of this is over and I look back on this part of my life, I want to look at it with satisfaction, not regret. I want to be the person who says, "I stood up for myself and for what I believe in. I was strong in the face of adversity, and I did what I thought was right. I had the courage to say no and hold true to what I believe in. It might seem wrong to you, but what is wrong for you might be right for me. People have the right to make their own decisions and come to their own conclusions in a free and open society, and last I checked, Canada was glorious and free."

In the future, maybe Chris and I will return to New Zealand. Maybe one day we will take the long flight across the Pacific Ocean to the magical little island where I long to live. One day I will land on those shores again and I will feel those same feelings I had when I first got there. I'll get off the plane in Queenstown and revisit those places I used to frequent when I was there. It won't be the same, because life is not the same anymore, but it will be similar. I'll buy a tent and drive to Twelve Mile Delta campground, where the Tūī in the woods will wake me up in the morning, and I will traverse the rivers with Chris in pursuit of the golden nugget that will make our fortune. We will walk in Queenstown Gardens, alongside Lake Wakatipu, marvelling over the fact that we finally made it back. The view of the city will be as magnificent as it always was, in the sunny daylight of the summer. The water will be blue and clear, Ben Lomond will stand remarkably alongside The Remarkables, and the TSS Earnslaw's steam engine will continue its chug-chug, cruising along the lake to Walter Peak High Country Farm. We will hike along the Te Araroa trail, the 3000 km trail that spans New Zealand. We will finally elope on the slowly disappearing glacier and have a lovely honeymoon in our own backyard. We will go on bicycle wine tours as if they only existed for us and camp along the bubbling Kawarau River. We will learn all about the Māori culture and find a way to uphold the values of whakapapa and whanaungatanga in our lives. We will find peace and comfort in the stillness of our lives in New Zealand.

For now, I have to learn how to go with the flow, live in the moment, and not worry too much about what the future holds. I can't change the past, and the future can change too easily to try and control it. I have had to learn how to relax and listen to the sound of the Ottawa River, where the birds sing in the morning and the sunlight crackles through the mist along the banks of the water. It might seem to an outsider that I gave up my security for the unknown, but the process of finding my truth has been more than rewarding.

Regardless of whether or not I ever make it back to New Zealand, I have come to realize it is more important to live in the present moment rather than worry about how my future is going to turn out. When I first met Chris, I told him my five-year plan for my life. This made him laugh and he said to me, "Plans change."

When he told me this, it annoyed me slightly and I thought he was being a bit of a jerk at the time, but now I have realized I have to accept that my plans have changed and it is okay they did. No matter how much my 'plans' change, I have to continue to trust myself and follow my intuition because I know it will lead me down the right path. I've come to understand how important it is for me to stay genuine and remain true to the path I have decided to follow.

I believe people participating in the healthcare system have a right to be fully informed and the right to choose the medical procedure they feel is best for them and their situation. In my opinion, it is not ethical to coerce or bribe a patient into medical procedures they don't want or agree to have. I feel the government has no business meddling in the healthcare field and dictating which medical procedures its population must have in order to participate in society.

Furthermore, I know medical information is supposed to be confidential—between one's doctor and oneself—and the process of showing health care records to access different facilities like theatres, gyms, or restaurants, seems, at the very least, an invasion of medical privacy. I don't want to show my waitress my health care records, she really has no business knowing anything about my medical history.

It has been said that everyone has a slightly different version of the truth, but I do believe we all want similar things out of life. I believe we all want to be treated with kindness and respect and so I do my best to follow the golden rule. I believe it is important to stay true to yourself and be genuine, even if it means showing up and admitting you were wrong. I believe people should be allowed to follow their own path through life while exercising free will. I believe in the sovereignty of the human body and mind. I believe people should have privacy when it comes to their medical decisions and I will advocate for my patients to have these things.

I am not happy about the past two years of chaos or the situations I have had to face in regard to my career, but my desire to align myself with my inner truth and follow my heart has led me down a path of learning and discovery where I have found peace in my life.

My immediate plan is simple: move forward by taking care of myself properly and getting enough exercise, water, healthy food, and time outside having fun and doing things that make me happy. I want to laugh and play with my friends and try not to take life too seriously because it's an adventure to be alive.

My desire is for people to read my story and understand where I am coming from and why I made the decisions I have made. I want them to know the sacrifices I have made were not easy or enjoyable for me. It would have been way easier for me to go along with the crowd, but in the words of C.S. Lewis in *The Screwtape Letters*,

"Indeed, the safest road to Hell is the gradual one—the gentle slope, soft underfoot, without sudden turnings, without milestones, without signposts."

I'm not sure where I will be in two, five, or ten years from now, but for now, I can be found in the forest or by the river, reading books and writing in my journal about how to solve all of the problems of the world.

REBECCA FLORIS

Rebecca began writing stories when she was nine years old and has always aspired to write and publish books. She achieved a print journalism diploma before embarking upon her career path as a nurse, where she graduated with outstanding academic achievement in 2013. She has held many different jobs in Canada and New Zealand and acquired many different certifications, but none of which have brought her as much joy as reading and writing have done. Her many hobbies include singing, playing piano, hiking, camping, kay-aking, cooking, and kittens. She has spent the last several summers by the Ottawa River, surrounded by the magic of whitewater, and she continues to pursue adventure at every opportunity.

This chapter is dedicated to my child, for whom this fight means everything to me.

I would also like to thank the following people: mom and dad for your unwavering love and support, my best friend, Chris, for supporting me and encouraging me to follow my dreams, and my brothers and sisters and their families, whom I have always loved dearly, and my grandparents, who always believed in my dreams to be a writer.

A special mention also goes out to the wonderful people I met in the South Island, New Zealand, and the amazing raft guides and friends I met on the Ottawa River- thank you for making me feel welcome and showing me the true meaning of hospitality and friendship.

Never forget you are free.
Free to say Yes.
Free to say No.
Free to choose your path
And do what is right for you.
Free to be yourself.
Free to speak your truth.
Free to be here.
Human.
Free.
With all my love,

Rebecca Floris

Chapter Five

THE FORTITUDE OF MY GUT INSTINCT

Rosanna Di Fiore

Racist. Misogynist. Unacceptable views. Should we tolerate these people who take up space?

These words cut like a knife. Mr. Prime Minister, how dare you call me names, undermine my intelligence, and question my belonging? You demonized me and turned the rest of the country against me. Legacy media, how dare you choose not to hold him accountable for his hateful spew? Instead, you printed headlines like, "I have no empathy left for the willfully unvaccinated. Let them die." You had the audacity to run a *poll* which found that many Canadians wanted jail time for the unvaxxed. This is hard to conceptualize. It is vicious, and it is a heartless attack. I have been on the pill for most of my life. Not the type you might think. But the type that served me almost as a life support. Imagine, being a lifetime customer of Big Pharma, and suddenly I wasn't welcome in my own world. I was disqualified from belonging because I questioned the science behind the "jab." I was already both a victim and a survivor of the limitations and side effects big pharma had ascribed to me. This time around, I chose common sense to be my cure.

***

Hashimoto's autoimmune disease. A life sentence of medication. It was a hard pill to swallow in my twenties. For three decades, I searched for answers. But all I kept being told was that I would be on thyroid medication for the rest of my life. So I went about my life without a reason to believe that medical answers were missing. The near entirety of my adult life was spent facing off with an array of symptoms like panic attacks, insomnia, severe exhaustion, a foggy brain, weight loss, cold hands, arthritis-like achiness in my joints, chronic constipation, forgetfulness, irrational anxiety, and a racing heart that could go up to one hundred twenty beats per minute out of nowhere, sometimes prompting the panic attacks that would wake me in the middle of the night and have me rushed to the hospital. I did the medication dance for years, scared of what would happen if I went off this pill, and all the while, my symptoms got worse. At times I felt judged and unheard. I felt so vulnerable within my own body and so frustrated in the offices of doctor after doctor and specialist after specialist, that I had finally concluded with certainty that they just didn't have the answers. The medical establishment has always been propagated as being the authority on health. Yet chronic illness is at an all-time high, and millions of Canadians are sick or dealing with mystery symptoms every day of their lives. I am one of them. Let me be clear that I revere good medical science. There are incredibly gifted and talented doctors, surgeons, nurses, scientists, chemists, all doing profound work in both conventional and alternative medicine. I thank God every day for these compassionate healers. However, like any human pursuit, medical science is still a work in progress. It is multi-faceted. It's constantly evolving, so theories that one day seem like the be-all and end-all can be revealed the next day to be obsolete. It is not a one size fits all solution. The truth of the matter is: Science doesn't have every answer, and Science is not God.

By my late thirties, I was sick and tired of feeling sick and tired. And so I took matters into my own hands and took an active role in my health. I continued my quest for medical freedom by researching and investigating and asking many more questions. I soon discovered that thyroid medicine does nothing for the thyroid itself. It doesn't eliminate hypothyroidism. The thyroid stays underactive, the medication only helps mask the symptoms and in my case, makes them worse. Unfortunately, there appear to be severe flaws in our system and a lot of confusion in the medical world about what's causing what. And the misdiagnoses are rampant. If chronic suffering were understood, the epidemic of mystery illness would not be plaguing the population the way it is today. Being part of the experimental fad in both conventional and alternative medicine all these years, I discovered that they don't become popular because they work. They become popular because of vested interests—power and money behind them—that allow these trends to grow, rather than seek alternative and effective solutions. All this at the expense of the patient's well-being, who is told to accept "the science." The question for me remained: which "science"?

The fortitude of my gut instinct has enlightened me to seek medical freedom and take back control of my life by trusting in my body's own healing capabilities. You are a reliable source of information just by heeding your own instincts and experiences. You don't need to outsource all of your thinking to the government, to the media, or to anyone who tells you to do so. When something feels off, I always trust the signs. I never allow fact-checkers to override my intuition. This is the type of knowing that has saved my life. It advised me to realize there is no quick fix, there is no magic pill or jab. Health and wellness is a personal lifestyle, a path, a journey. And unfortunately, there is no formula for this. It's usually a realization that drains us. At some point in the journey, you realize you speak a language of suffering the world doesn't try to understand and you must walk to your own salvation. It's a lonely path, but the pain-filled days provide you with courage. I did not want to be stuck with this fate. I no longer believed what I was being told to be true, that the drugs had been caring for my thyroid. I was finally empowered to ameliorate my thyroid condition. I found the truth about what was causing my condition and I was able to reclaim control over my own health. I learned how to listen to my body and know what is right for me.

***

It was March 2021. I was standing in a long line which wrapped around St. Michael's Hospital, with the elderlies in our family all frantically waiting to be called in to get their shot which I booked for them. A random homeless person walked straight in my face and shouted, "it's a hoax, get out of the line and save yourselves." I turned to my father, and in a nervous laugh I said, "I hope this guy does not know something we don't know." Deep down inside, I got a strange feeling. The first question that popped into my mind at the moment was: Why didn't covid wipe out the homeless population yet? My gut was telling me something. Maybe I should investigate the real safety of this injection for myself.

I was fearless, and I began researching extensively and asking a lot of questions that professionals could not answer confidently because they had no real answers or real evidence. I set up appointments with all my caregivers. Except for my naturopath, all my conventional doctors were trying to convince me to take the jab. "Look," one of them said to me on a virtual phone call, "I wasn't going to get it, but I did. You'll have to eventually, too, if you want to do anything." End of explanation! My next appointment was in person.

I went in armed with all my research. "Doctor," I said as I sat across from her, "people with autoimmune conditions are being told to receive the Covid-19 vaccine. *However*, it doesn't mean they should, right? Are you aware that no data is currently available on the safety of Covid-19 vaccines for people with autoimmune conditions? Autoimmune diseases generally involve difficulties with the immune system turning itself off, so any stimulation of the immune system can sometimes lead to a flare of disease. All this is on the Ontario government website. I also know for a fact that the hospitals are asking people as they sign in to get their shots if they have an autoimmune, and bringing them into another room just in case. Why?" She sat there listening attentively as she always did and then said: "yes, it might be risky and you raise good points. My own son suffered pericarditis."

"OMG!!" I uttered in shock. "I am so sorry to hear that. Is he okay?"

"Yes, but he needs to be closely monitored and has been on meds." She explained this matter-of-factly and was seemingly calm about it all. I was speechless and sat in total disbelief, witnessing firsthand my own doctor's personal testimonial on vaccine injury, yet here she was, giving me her blessing in an utterly mute manner. As she appeared to agree with my position, she continued to say, "I am so sorry. I can't grant you a medical exemption because I fear getting flagged and stripped of my license."

I left her office that day shaken up and almost in tears. She knew my health story and she knew perfectly well that if I took the jab, especially as an autoimmune patient I might be harmed. Yet here she was turning my body over to "state care." I felt hopeless ... I felt hopeless because she no longer had the power to advocate for me as her patient. She knew perfectly well that the foundation of medicine was built on informed consent. Risks, benefits, and alternative treatments are always explained, because the same medical treatment that saves one person can hurt, disable, or kill another person. From a tablet, to a surgery, to an injection. I believe that in her heart of hearts, she knew that it was wrong. Wrong on so many levels! I was so distraught by it all. And I asked myself so many times why no one was questioning the College of Physicians and Surgeons of Ontario (CPSO) who were threatening doctors. Why were our trusted doctors and our healthcare system, which hold a unique position of trust with the public and have a professional responsibility to their patients, being mandated by the government to follow their orders without any discretion of their own? Why, if they chose to advocate for their patients, were they threatened with an investigation by the CPSO, including potential disciplinary action?

Vaccine hesitancy was very prevalent in the beginning, but inevitably began to dwindle as time went on and vaccination was positioned as the popular thing to do. Cognitive dissonance started taking over the mass minds and it kept running deep. I remember asking so many people why they decided to get vaccinated when I knew perfectly well they did not want to take it. Most gave me the same response, "well, my doctor would tell me if I should not get it . . ." But unfortunately, they did not realize that doctors could not say a word because what they worked for all their lives was being held ransom. Many doctors were made an example of, so that many would self-censor. So many, along with immunologists, lost their licenses or got backlashes for stating their opinion or experience with early treatments. I kept questioning my doctors why they were not given the same power as big pharma to try to save the world from dying. Wouldn't we want to welcome as many solutions as possible to the table, especially since the vaccines were experimental themselves? These doctors truly wanted to help in the crisis, and they had no incentive to risk everything for nothing after spending so many years in school. There was no doubt in my mind that we had reached a point where our Canadian Public Health was captured by the pharmaceutical industry, telling the nation's physicians and pharmacists not to use generic medicines, even if they worked.

As time went on, the narrative kept changing. No real data, just one big experiment being tested on the population, all sold by a pharmaceutical company with the biggest lawsuits in the world! How was I supposed to just take this "risk" and hope for the best? I was basically being told to sell everything I own, put it all in one stock that has no track record and just trust the "science" on this! The only difference here was that the gamble was on my health. The health I had put so much work into all my life. If you dared to question "the science," you were labelled as anti-science and an anti-vaxxer, even though the root of all science is in the art of questioning. The fact that questioning had become so taboo sent a chill up my spine. The big shocker for me was when the CDC decided to change the definition of the word "vaccine" by eliminating the word "immunity" and replacing it with the word "protection." This made-up new rule made it easier for them to explain why herd immunity was never being reached, even though we were being told our population was ninety percent vaccinated! And what happened to natural immunity? Yet many doctors followed the media and trusted businessmen, instead of reading the entirety of the data, including that in preprints. Research conducted by pharmaceutical companies and approved by people with a financial stake in the underlying product is not science. It's marketing. At this point, the great push for *vaccine* became very questionable. Why was it only about an experimental *vaccine*?

As difficult as my decision was, I had to also accept the hard fact that going forward, I would be treated as a second-class citizen. Most would be able to carry on in society, but only if they could show their proof of vaccination papers. I, too, wanted to be able to download my digital proof of immunity, but all I was served was proof of exclusion. A lifetime of advocating for my own health, and suddenly I was vulnerable and alone once again.

I felt scared for the collective, but most importantly, I was terrified for my loved ones—especially my children. I remember one evening vividly. I was sitting at the dinner table with my family, feeling sick to my stomach as they discussed getting their vaccines when their turn was up. My voice and opinion reached a boiling point that eventually drowned in the food we were eating—for the first time in my role as a mother and wife, I was powerless, and it did not matter what I had to say. They wholeheartedly trusted the authorities on this one, not their health-fanatic, loving mother who had a proven track record of doing her research. This time, I was irrelevant. I resigned my position and did not bother arguing. I had no choice. I took each day as it came. Full of anger and emotional exhaustion. "Mom, why are you upset all the time," they would ask, and my only response was, "Look at all these facts! I am trying to show you why, please open your eyes!" They continued to discard my evidence and carried on with their day. All I could do going forward was pray harder every day, pray that they would be okay, and pray the nightmare we faced would end immediately.

The only person I had a chance to protect was my youngest son, given his unique health situation and young age. He needed to be vaccinated in order for him to play hockey. Everyone on his team was vaccinated and so were most of his friends. I was adamant about my decision, even if it meant my son would become unpopular and be setting an unprecedented example as assistant captain of his team, now playing from the sidelines of his home rather than the hockey arenas with his teammates. This tested my marriage to the core. I threatened to leave if anyone dared to take my son to get vaccinated. For weeks, I cried myself out of tears. There were many times I wanted to run away from it all and come back when the nightmare was over. But I stuck it out. And over time, as the two unjabbed members of our entire family, we thankfully gained the respect and love we deserved for the choice I made on our behalf. Home was still a safe haven. Societally speaking, my son and I had become victims of abuse. We both experienced the kind of psychological violence that cuts deep into the veins and causes bruising on a great emotional level that is undeniably cruel. The government and the media manipulated the masses to become intolerant of, and even to hate, the unvaccinated. I will never forget all the people who wished for death, sickness, discrimination against, and/or punishment of their unvaccinated neighbours and fellow citizens. The hate was created purposefully for us to be weakened through division, and for them, the government, to remain powerful. And the nightmare only continued . . . there was no waking up from it.

In December 2021, I could sense something was off when my son returned home from school and I asked him how his day was. As I probed him a little more he said, "Mom, I got kicked out of McDonald's today!" he said nervously, as if he had done something wrong.

"Whaaaaat?" I remarked. "What do you mean?"

"They told me I was not allowed to stay and eat with my friends because I did not have my papers."

A sense of paralysis washed over me. My breath shallowed and my heart beat faster as the full magnitude of my son's experience hit me. My words became muffled and it felt like I was unable to speak, but I managed to squeak out, "So what did you do?"

"I left, mom. They said to buy my food and leave the restaurant because I was not allowed to eat there."

"Did you leave by yourself?" I asked.

"No, my friend came with me, the others stayed."

This feeling of a hard kick in the stomach I received on that day will never leave me. My son had just been humiliated and society was normalizing this behaviour. That day, my son had been segregated into the "medical haves" and "medical have nots" of society. They were making it high-fashion to be vaccinated, and if you didn't receive your vaccine "star," you could not attend any of society's extracurriculars. I felt like I could die of a broken heart.

Thankfully, the Christmas holidays rolled around and it felt like an opportunity to give my son a break from the social ostracization that no thirteen-year-old should ever have to experience. On one particular day, I was trying to console my son, who was feeling totally isolated and segregated from his peers, as he watched them be able to do all the things he wanted to do but was no longer welcome to. He turned to me and said, "Mom, why does it feel like we are the only ones stuck inside forever?" He was reeling from the fact that we were not allowed to travel, go to a restaurant, the movies, or watch the Raptors or Leafs games live in the Scotiabank Arena. *How do I even explain this as a mother?* I thought to myself, feeling utterly hopeless, with blow after blow to my son's heart. Then he said, "Maybe we can get tickets to go to the Christmas market this year since it's outdoors." A sigh of hope came over me, and I couldn't purchase tickets fast enough because I just wanted my son to have some sense of normalcy in his life and a distraction from the pain.

"For sure we will be allowed," I said, "It's outside, why wouldn't we?!" But as I went to purchase our tickets, my stomach dropped when I saw the covid banner flash at the top of the website stating you *must be fully vaccinated to attend our outdoor Christmas Market.* "You've gotta be f'en kidding!" I yelled. My trucker's mouth kept unleashing eighteen-wheels worth of expletive language. These were the only words that could numb my pain and truly express my utter fricken astonishment at how fricken unbelievable this world had become.

"What's wrong mom, why can't we go? It's outside, so why won't they allow us in? We will have our masks on. I promise I won't take mine off!" I felt like I had been stabbed in the heart. It felt like no matter where we turned, we were being squeezed. We were being seen as lepers, manipulated, and banned from society. How could this make sense to anyone? How could this be okay to anyone? The depth of pain that we experienced is something I will never forget.

Being ostracized is extremely painful and does something to a person. With every door that closed on us, every notice, bulletin or banner that announced our disinvitation, every snarky comment and outright verbal abuse sent an electric shock right through me, especially when it affected my kids.

Having to call another parent to request that their child stop covid bullying my son for not being vaccinated is something I never thought I would be doing as a parent, yet there I was. I was full of rage that day, and I did not hold back. I gave this mother no fluff and no small talk just the straight goods.

"I'm sorry my son has done this. I guess it's our fault because we told our kids not to hang out with unvaccinated kids," she had the audacity to say to me.

"Oh really? What if I told you I could easily call the school and report this as a bullying act?" I responded.

"Oh, I'm so sorry you are so upset, and I don't want to pry on why you haven't vaccinated your son yet, but I want you to know they say it's safe and effective and it helps us protect one another," she continued.

"Guess what?" I said, "Being safe and protected vs. feeling safe and protected are two different things, and the reason for not getting my son vaccinated is between myself, my husband, and my doctor, just like it has always been. The fear-mongering campaign, in my opinion, has created this "right" that the vaccinated can use to feel protected from other people. Almost making it a democratic right. They have normalized one's fear that they would die of the virus if they did not get vaccinated. All with zero proof that our children are really the ones at risk. One death of covid is too much to bear. Deaths from vaccines? No one seems to care. So I really hope you have a serious talk with your son, so I don't have to call the school." End of conversation.

After this day, I realized I had become a warrior living and fighting the good fight in a horror movie called "The Powerful Weapons of Mass Deception." The exhaustion from being in defence mode for what felt like twenty-four hours a day was enough to bring me to my knees. I didn't need people to think like me. I just needed them to think. Critically. The evidence was mounting that I had made the right decision for my son and me. Hundreds of thousands of vaccine injuries and deaths had gone unreported. All with the convenient disclaimer "total immunity without accountability" if something goes wrong. My eyes opened wider and wider as I watched big pharma make an effort to conceal their evidence for seventy-five years, which was thankfully overridden by a Texas court judge, and they were ordered to make their clinical trials fully public by September 2022. There was enough white paper evidence for everyone to see - a roughly ninety-nine percent survival rate and the Covid-19 vaccine benefits are not proven to outweigh the risks, especially for children and young, healthy adults. I wanted to scream it from the rooftop to anyone who would listen. But my pleading voice remained silent in most of the ears I tried to open. People would rather dismiss empirical evidence before their very eyes than contemplate how dreadfully we were taken advantage of in the name of control, under the guise of health. They preferred to look the other way and focus on happier things rather than "politics." It's all too hard to fathom how evidence seems to mean nothing these days, so long as government-paid doctors say otherwise. Still, I held onto hope that the truth would prevail.

In the meantime, I began to contemplate ways that would allow us to participate in an underground society. I would not sit idle, especially since this affected my child so deeply. I began to make phone calls. Luckily, I was able to find my son a spot on an unvaccinated soccer team. One of my best friends introduced me to her son's coach and told me that he would be welcomed with open arms. As the coach welcomed us to the team, he had one thing to add, "If you want your son to play on this team, you have to be willing to drive an hour away to a region that allows unvaccinated youth access to indoor facilities. It's the only facility we could find that accepts our kids."

"I don't care if I have to drive five hours," I remarked, "I am just grateful that my son found his people." All I wanted was for my son to feel accepted again and get back to playing a sport that he loved. As we made our way on the brutal wintery road of the 401 that first night of practice, all I could remember was the excitement in my son's voice as he laughed and giggled with the other two boys we were carpooling with. I was elated.

Help continued coming to me in different directions, this time from a very unexpected group of people and an unexpected series of events. Omicron showed up like "karma" and changed everything! The vaccinated were now put in the penalty box with the unvaccinated. They no longer held the power they were told they would hold if they just *got vaccinated*. And blessed was this day in January 2022. Who could have imagined that a group of Canucks and their transport trucks would try to save the day by travelling thousands of kilometres in their transport trucks to meet our government in Ottawa? It was truly a *deus ex machina* moment. With each passing day, streets across the country were lined on either side with thousands upon thousands of people, children, mothers, fathers, and grandparents, from all ethnicities honking their horns, waving their flags, crying tears of hope, and welcoming the truckers as they passed through their cities from coast to coast. Every night I would listen to the trucker radio app for inspiration. The most uplifting voices were those of innocent children expressing their gratitude to the truckers as they drove across our land through the treacherous roads of Canadian winter. "Good night truckers, thank you for fighting for our freedoms," they would say every night.

As I told my husband I was going to Ottawa, he pleaded, "please don't go to Ottawa. Go to the protest when they cross Ontario if you want, but not Ottawa, I don't want you getting stuck there," he explained. "Oh, and by the way," he continued, "please don't make the news!"

Off I went to attend the first protest in my life! It was -20°C that day, and there I stood, all bundled up with two of my closest mom friends, waving our flags, talking, and taking selfies with courageous truckers waiting to join the line. "Some of us are vaccinated and some of us are not," one explained. "But this is not why we are joining this fight. We are fighting for the freedom of our country and our basic rights," he said.

As we all divulged our personal stories on why we were fighting like hell, we were saddened and shocked by our tellings. By the time we all finished telling our stories, none of us knew what to say. We all knew what was wrong with the situation and stood there in the numb collective trauma we had been forced into, knowing we were powerless. We had all been through a lot while everyone around us lived life without a clue of what this side of history was going through. The psychological war had brought us all to our knees and this was our time to unite. The honking and screaming of the word "Freedom" started getting really intense as we stood over the 401 overpass, waving our flags as the convoy of trucks started rolling in like thunder from across this great nation.

"OMG!" I yelled from my living room, "I made the news!" There I was with my friend, front and centre on my television screen. The "Freedom Convoy" was the headline story of the day. "I guess it was a good day!" said my husband, laughing. "Congratulations!" Indeed, it was the best day ever. The truckers and protestors occupied the nation's capital for nearly three weeks thereafter before being forcefully pushed out by the police.

I don't care what anyone says, the convoy changed the trajectory of the country's mandates. And their presence made a huge impact worldwide, with convoys sparking up all over the globe to fight for their freedoms, too. With great intention, I became part of The Freedom Movement. It was certainly deemed unpopular. But us mothers *did not* care. We didn't care because we knew we were the ones asking the question that doctors themselves could not answer.

"Why is the covid vaccine uptake amongst kids so low, and given that it is so low, why have they not been mandated in schools?"

Dr. Moore's answer in March 2022: "It is a new vaccine. Some would like more experience with it." Yet millions of parents obeyed the Public Health officials without question because they trusted them. So why are pharmaceutical companies still seeking emergency use of this vaccine for children? Why give our children this mRNA vaccine if they have a higher chance of drowning than dying of covid? Why try to entice them with a Polkaroo mascot campaign and free pizza and ice cream? Morally and ethically wrong on all levels. We *did not* care because we knew there was a lack of credibility and ethics. We *did not* care because we were the ones to notice that "science" was no longer about public health, but rather about politics, once it started to differ by geographical areas. We *did not* care because we knew we saw what many could not see. We were the ones to Hold the Line.

One of the things that has stuck with me during my time in this movement, was my vision of my kids and their kids getting to live free of any mandates, control, division, and hatred. I was fighting for them. I want to teach my kids that their rights are not gifts from the government. The government does not own them. I believe in health autonomy and health sovereignty as principles. I will never give up my values or way of life because of the evil of the world. Rotten fruit falls by itself, and so will the evils of our time. Luckily, my rage was able to transcend to resolve. My fear submitted to conviction.

It was time to shield my family again, so I pulled up a seat at our dinner table one night, feeling uninvited, as I pleaded, "please don't turn a blind eye this time. These vaccines do not protect against Omicron. Do your research, the efficacy wanes. Please don't fall for the 'Boosted' loyalty program. Why get boosted without doing blood work first? The whole 'follow without question' mentality makes me sick," I implored! "Just because you see the advertising sign on the

401 telling you to 'BOOST UP' does not mean you should obey. What you should be asking is why there is no disclaimer! What happened to 'This medication may not be right for you, check with your doctor first?' What happened to *this is our shot* with doses one and two? And when was it normal to take the same flu shot four times in one year or less?" Thank the heavens, this time they listened. In fact, my entire family listened this time. For the first time in a long time, I had tears of joy. Thank you, God!

Once again, life returned to (somewhat) normal—for most. The unvaccinated were still held prisoners in the largest prison in the world: Canada. Unable to leave, unless they escaped. Unable to board a plane or a train within their own country. Most had little idea how we were still fighting the big fight behind the scenes. My son was still not allowed to play hockey because the hockey organization decided to hold onto the mandates regardless of the provinces dropping them. The largest hockey organization in Canada was given the power by our government, and they took advantage of it. "No one is putting others at risk anymore! And shame on any business who is perpetuating this lie," I stated in my letter to them.

To all the parents on his team who voted for my son to *not* return to the game after March 1st: I will never forget, and I hope your conscience cripples you for your awful wrongdoing that had no logic. You have no explanation to stand on, you simply chose to exclude him. And if you didn't acknowledge and apologize, you are to blame. Even if you were quiet or said to yourself, "well, what can I do?" You are to blame. It was no longer about science. Perhaps it never was—but it certainly became all about control. A sovereign nation starts with a sovereign individual. And so, the constant assaults proved their worth and evil wishes were no longer able to enslave me. Canada was no longer recognizable as the land my parents and three-month-old-me risked it all for, as they left their native land with the diaspora of boat people from Italy. Never in a million years would I think I might be telling my grandkids one day, "back in '22, your grandmother and your uncle had to escape Canada." I couldn't believe what had become of the country I loved so dearly, but I would no longer allow these atrocities to impact my family and me. Sovereignty is our birthright.

The power of food, lifestyle, and mindfulness is true medicine that should not be undermined. The phrase 'health is wealth' has never been so true as in the past two years. Viewing the world through printed headlines is a dangerous, slippery slope. I choose to write my own headlines and move in a different direction that leads me in my truth, fiercely, unashamed, and unapologetically! No one has all the answers, but we should always have questions that people are allowed to talk about.

I want my children to understand that no matter how big a bully is, even if that bully is a figure of authority like the government, you must stand up to them, especially when they compromise our ability to live peacefully and freely in our society. The government works for us, the people, not the other way around. It is our responsibility to be democratic and not the responsibility of the government to make us democratic. An informed citizen will always be the biggest threat to the system. You must call out the wrong, even when it's scary and unpopular to do so. Even when the whole world is condemning it. Tyranny can only exist through fear, silence, and compliance. We must all stand up, speak up, and never comply with government overreach. May it never be said of me that I was silent in the face of fear, and in so doing, passed on the battle to my children.

ROSANNA DI FIORE

Rosanna is a proud mother, wife, daughter, sister, aunt and community volunteer. She considers herself a conservative woman living her life as a traditional wife, homemaker and provider in a traditional marriage. Cooking barefoot is only one of her superpowers. She *happily* serves her family and often loves to brag about being CEO of her home more than any other title given to her in her past corporate life. She believes there is no more important role in society than motherhood. Her three children and husband are the fuel to her fire in this world. Cut from a different cloth, Rosanna's grit, determination, integrity, and passion for what's right and true makes her refreshingly real in such a curated world. A fierce protector, Rosanna is courageous enough to be viewed as unpopular as she advocates for who and what is nearest and dearest to her heart. Rosanna gives back to her community generously with her time by bringing people together, helping the less fortunate, and stimulating the human spirit. The fortitude of her gut instinct has been her biggest blessing in life. It's helped her become fearless and unstoppable. It freed her from the existential fears and worries of the present time.

For my children, I love you all to infinity and beyond.

To my husband, for his unconditional and unwavering love. Thank you for you for choosing me, every day and always. I thank you for building a strong family unit based on hard work and loyalty. I thank you for your selfless commitment of always putting our family first before yourself. I love your motto. Family. First, Always.

I would like to humbly acknowledge my mother, who has instilled within me the ability to discern and to think critically. And how crucial those things are to living an authentic life. She has taught me not to be impressed by money, degrees, and titles, but to be impressed by humility, generosity, integrity, and kindness. And to my father, who taught me that you can never change things by fighting the existing reality; the only way to change something is to build a new reality. He has taught me that if you never step up, you will never step forward. The secret to happiness is freedom, and the secret to freedom is courage.

I honour all the incredible parents who have been fighting the good fight with me from day one.

May you never allow fear to cripple your good judgment & critical thinking!

Rosanna Di Fiore

Chapter Six

MAKING PLANS

Meaghan Penney

In the absolute darkest moments of my life, I have a deep need to take a deep breath, bird's-eye view the situation, and make a plan. I ask myself . . .

What can I control?

What can I change?

Where can I make this situation a positive?

What can I do right now?

This hasn't always been something I have done, but it's something I learned to do during one particularly dark time in my life. It couldn't have been more needed once 2020 showed up.

But let's start at the beginning . . .

February 23, 2016

The elephant in this room is taking all the oxygen. I can't breathe, and it's just standing there like a selfish asshole taking all the space and all of the oxygen.

I heard what he said, "I am not in love with you anymore. I want a divorce."

The passive-aggressive, hurt little child in me wanted to respond, "we aren't even legally married," and roll my eyes. The shocked me wanted me to curl into the fetal position and cry until I woke up from this nightmare.

I have to leave.
I need air . . . I need space.
What did he just say . . . You know what he said.
I can't do this.
What about the kids?
What about our plans?
Where will I live?
What about my business?
You don't love him anymore anyway!
I wanted to at least TRY.
We have tried . . .
I need a drink.
I need my mom.
No, I need a drink.

March 20. 2016

I'm not one hundred percent sure I even know what day it is today. I know the kids are home, so it's not a school day. I can hear them in the kitchen rummaging for snacks and yelling at their video games. How much did I drink last night? It must have been the whole bottle because I woke up on the bathroom floor. Okay Meaghan, on the count of three, we're going to stand up and look in the mirror. *Do we have to do THAT?* Yes, we have to do that.

One . . . no not yet.

Two . . . I said not yet.

Three . . . I can't

GET UP NOW!

I know what I'm going to see, and I'm not ready to face myself. It's been almost a month, and he's serious this time. This is it. We're over. Eighteen years of my life for what? I did everything he asked me to, and he still left. I gave up on myself. I walked away from myself. **I complied**. I did what I was told. I agreed with everything that was said. I stifled my thoughts. I quieted my opinions. I sacrificed so much and buried who I was so I didn't make anyone uncomfortable. Who am I kidding? He was the only uncomfortable one, I left everyone behind who accepted me and loved me, and allowed myself to become someone I wasn't. I was a shell of a human. I was no longer Meaghan Reid. I was a mom, a compliant little wife, a cleaner and cook, and apparently not a good one at that. I had willingly just given every single part of myself over. It hadn't happened all at once, though.

Every fight, every slammed door, every dish thrown, every insult, every hole in the wall, every threat of leaving, every time money was taken away. Piece by piece, bit by bit, every single day for eighteen years, I had shed the smallest slivers of myself. I hid myself away. Quiet as a mouse.

Don't say what's on your mind.

Don't be too much,

Don't drink! Put that cigarette out!

Did you work out today? You can't gain too much weight!

For what? For this? To be a broken, hungover human on a bathroom floor? Who the fuck am I? I don't think I'm even sure anymore. I do know I am better than this. I'm pretty sure I was made for more.

Ok, I'm standing up now.

And there I was, emotionless eyes, hollow cheeks, pale complexion, and the blackest bags I've ever seen.

No, this is not who we are.

I can literally still remember this day like it happened yesterday. It's seared right into my soul, and maybe that's a good thing. Because it was the day I knew that I needed to come back to myself and that I would never ever give a piece of myself away to make anyone else comfortable again. I had things to say, I had opinions, I had ideas ... brilliant ones at times too! I was smart, I was kind of funny, I was a little bit witchy, I can cook like your gramma used to. I have a brilliant mind when it comes to other people's businesses, I'm creative ...

The list just started to unfurl in front of me ... oh yes, I remember you.

Hello!

I've missed you.

Same.

Let's go take a shower, put on some make-up and then make a plan.

May 16, 2019

"Mom . . . I need your help. I'm bleeding. I think something is wrong with the baby."

One thing is for sure, I don't care how old I get, I'm pretty sure I will always need my mom. She arrived so quickly, but as I sat on the porch waiting for her, it felt like forever. Getting pregnant so quickly seemed like a dream come true for Jerry and I, we had literally only decided after our honeymoon in February that we wanted to have a baby, and in March, the stick gave us two lines. We told our families just one week ago that we were expecting, because waiting until you're thirteen weeks is what you're supposed to do. That's the "Safe Zone." We were in the clear. Except we weren't.

The doctor said, "I'm so sorry Mrs. Penney, the fetus didn't make it. It's showing that it hasn't been viable since week eight."

What did he just say? Eight weeks?

That was five weeks ago?

We had tests done. We did bloodwork.

I can't breathe.

Did I just scream?

What's wrong with Jerry?

Why isn't he saying anything?

I want to see the ultrasound.

I need a drink.

NO! That is the LAST thing you need. You need to rest and be gentle with yourself.

I need to go shower.

Put on make-up.

And then I need to make a plan.

But first . . . I just need to cry for a little bit, okay?

Okay.

March 13, 2020

This room is so hot.

Why am I shaking?

Why can't I catch my breath?

What did the doctor just say?

I can't hear . . .

"It's time to be scared now. You can't work for a bit. You can't be around the public right now, Meaghan."

But I literally work in person with the public, what am I supposed to do? I'm three months pregnant. I have to pay my mortgage. I can't bird's-eye view this. How do I birds-eye view a pandemic? What is happening?

I drove back to the salon in a complete daze, still trying to process the words the doctor had said. "You are thirty-nine years old, you're pregnant, you just had a miscarriage nine months ago. You need to be safe right now until we get more information."

I have to call my clients. I have to reschedule them. I have to tell my boss.
OMG, my coworker's son has been sick all week.
What if I have it? I just saw my mom two days ago.
What if I gave it to her?
What if they close the grocery stores? I need to stock the fridge.
I have to call Jerry.
What if I die?
What happens to the boys if I die?
I need a will.

All of this went through my head in the twelve minutes it took me to get from the doctor's office to work. My head was pounding, my heart was racing.

Okay, deep breath.
Everything will be okay.
It's just a little vacation.
What's two weeks?
I could use the time to clean the house, organize the closets, wash the windows!
Yeah, just two weeks.
Everything will be okay in two weeks.

March 22, 2020

When was the last time I showered? Was it yesterday? I should probably shower, but my ass is glued to CP24 day and night. I need updates, I need to see the numbers, I need to stay safe, I have to protect the baby and my mom and my dad. I also need to pay the bills, how the heck are we going to pay the bills?

The fear and anxiety that coursed through my entire body during the early part of 2020 could have probably killed me if I'm being really honest. I didn't eat much, I barely slept, and I gobbled up the news every minute of the day. The state of the world was wreaking havoc on my nervous system. You know those electricity balls they have at the science centre that you just loved to touch when you were a kid? The ones that made your hair stand up and your body feel fuzzy; that's how I felt, every day . . . fuzzy and buzzy and unsettled.

I can't feel like this anymore.

I can't do this anymore.

I need to go shower, put on make-up.

And then I need to make a plan.

Okay!

May 5, 2020

Well, Universe . . . I guess we're starting that business after all.

Hairstylists are still considered "non-essential." We've been closed for two months now. I'm five months pregnant and the boys have moved home. *It's time for a plan!* I will not be reliant on government money. I had been skating around the idea of building a business for years, always bouncing from one idea to the next but never actually **doing** anything. My business coach was probably sick of my bullshit at this point.

What the hell was holding me back?

Fear, dude . . . it was always fear.

What if it flops?

But what if it's a success?

*What if it's **too** successful?*
What the . . . fuck do you mean, "too successful?!?"
How is this a fear we have?

My eyes roll back so far into my head, I'm pretty sure I can see behind me. I am ridiculous. When things go sideways, I make a plan! It's been two months, time for a plan!
Get out of bed.
Get dressed.
*Sit in front of the computer, and **let's GO!***

June 15, 2020

"I won't be coming back to the salon when the province opens back up next week." My hands were shaking as I said this to my boss. "I've started a business, and honestly, I only have two months left until this baby comes and It's just not worth it. I'll be referring my clients out and I won't be returning. Maybe after my mat leave, I'll come back." I was **never** going back. The pandemic was a lot of things, but I will always say it was secretly the largest blessing I have ever experienced. It forced me to make some very big moves in my life, and there's not a single one I regret, not even a little bit.

February 3, 2022

"Dude, my Facebook has been deactivated for violating community standards, I lost my Instagram, too." That was the voice message I sent to my best friend . . .

There were seventeen years' worth of content, memories, and photos on those platforms. Deactivated? For what? Because I shared my opinion? Because I shared my thoughts? Because I helped a movement that was sweeping this beautiful country? Yes, that was it.

You see, I was one of the administrators for the Freedom Convoy Facebook group, and we were **all** deactivated in the blink of an eye. Our sole job as admins was to make sure we removed any messages and posts that promoted hatred, division, racism, or violence from the page. We were to share posts that promoted unity, collect donations for convoy members, and share updates from two of the organizers on the road. That was the explicit ask of all admins, to be kind, spread love, share the truth, remove the hate, and that was what we did.

The day my account was deactivated was honestly the most eye-opening day for me. I think it was the day I woke **all the way up**. It was also the day that spiralled me down a hole so deep I wasn't sure how I would get back out. The hole I went down brought back all of the feelings, fears, and anger I had experienced in my past. The gaslighting, the emotional and mental abuse, all of it. Was this what PTSD felt like? I had been told previously in therapy that I had extreme PTSD from that time in my life, which never felt true to me, until that day.

I was silenced by a social media company because of my thoughts and opinions. I remember how it used to feel to not have a voice, I had worked so fucking HARD to regain my voice, and now I was being silenced again. Punished for speaking my truths. Punished for asking questions. Punished for disagreeing. Punished.

Spiral

Spiral

Spiral

It wasn't losing my social accounts that sent me spiralling, it was being silenced. Yes, losing all of that content and the memories was frustrating. But what was maddening was that with the click of a button I was erased from their platforms, as though I had never existed in that space ever. The ease with which some bot in a server room in Silicon Valley just went "*poof—you're gone!*" was defeating.

Had we not been through enough already? The lies. The lockdowns. The division. The isolation. Now . . . silenced.

Deep breath Meags, we can get through this.

Let's make a plan.

July, 2022

It's been awhile. So much more has happened. So many more lessons since the day my accounts were shut down.

- My husband lost his father.
- I crumbled beneath the weight of my grief mixed in with burn-out from these past two years.
- My business crumbled beneath the weight of my burnout.

There wasn't any more I could take. I said that out loud to myself in the mirror, "I cannot take anymore!"

No more grief

No more heartache

No more loneliness

No more loss

I stared at myself in the mirror some more and just cried.

How much can one person possibly take? I don't think I am strong enough for anymore.

The last two years had come crashing down on me like a tidal wave. We had collectively endured so much, hadn't we?

- The loss of friendships
- The divide in family units
- The turmoil in the world at large

So much fear, trauma, anxiety, loss, anger, and sadness.

Meaghan . . . you, my dear, have just endured the hardest two years of your life. Harder than anything you have ever faced. I want to remind you of a few things:

- *You gave birth to a beautiful baby girl in the midst of a global pandemic, completely isolated from your typical support system.*
- *You built a business all while you had sleepless nights with a newborn.*
- *You ran business meetings while you breastfed.*
- *You were strength and stability for your entire household.*
- *You maintained your positive outlook and unconditional love for humanity even when you were given all the evidence that people would turn their backs on you when you needed them the most.*
- *You held onto the faith and trust that the good guys will always win.*

I need you to take a moment to just breath.
You need some time.
You need to rest.

The last two years have been, at times, too much. I could make all the plans I wanted but really, I was just tired. I needed the reminder in this moment that after everything that I had been through over the last two and a half years . . . It was ok for the plan to simply be *rest*.

Present Day

People always say, "one day, you will look back on this moment and laugh," and I have always wanted to throat punch those people when I am in the moment. (*Sorry, not sorry, people.*)

There were times when I wondered how I could possibly look back on any of these experiences and laugh? Each one felt like it had consumed every fibre of me, I thought I had finally become so broken I wouldn't be able to put myself back together again. But the people really are right. As I sit here today on the grass surrounded by all of the food I am currently growing to feed my family for the year, I know I had to endure it all. I had to build this strength for this season in our lives.

We endure, we learn, we overcome, and then we take our lessons forward to the next phase of our life. I am finally able to look back on all of these experiences and my lessons with gratitude and a little giggle. Those moments did not actually break me. They all prepared me for the greatest lesson I would learn to date . . . that all of my power, all of my freedom, and my voice belonged only to me. The lesson that my life was my own. I had to collect all of the pieces of myself, that I gave away over my lifetime, hold them close and piece myself back together.

Now every day I remind myself . . .

- I am in charge of my life.
- I have everything I need.
- I can breathe.
- I am free.

MEAGHAN PENNEY

Meaghan Penney is a mom, wife, entrepreneur and proud member of the "Fringe Minority" here in Canada. She built a six-figure business in six months, while pregnant, after she was deemed "non-essential" in 2020. She faces every hurdle in her life head on and with the idea that everything is happening for us, not to us. She has worked hard these past two years to detach herself and her family from the system, all while still building the life she has always dreamed of. When Meaghan is not glued to her office chair supporting incredible business owners build their legacies, you can find her soaking up every sweet moment with her family, watching true crime documentaries, baking bread, and sitting in her vegetable garden.

To Jerry, my rock, my strength when I am weak, my love. Thank you for your never-ending love and support in everything I ever do.

To Jakub, Jeffrey, & Delilah, my reasons why. I love you all with everything in me. All three of you are a piece of my heart that lives outside of my body. Thank you for choosing me to be your mom.

To Sarah, thank you for your unconditional friendship. I'm not sure I could have navigated the last two years without you. I fucking love you, dude.

And to you reading this book. Thank you. Thank you for your support, and thank you for reading each of these stories. We hope these stories will never be lost and will live on forever so that no one forgets.

Love will always win

Chapter Seven

IMPROVEMENT = PROGRESS

Jeff Eichenberger

The game of golf has been an integral part of my life, both from a livelihood and spiritual perspective. I started playing when I was ten years old and started working at a course when I was thirteen. Now, I own two businesses that deal directly with the game. As I've gotten older and, dare say, wiser, I've become mildly obsessed with the difficulty. The sport requires the utmost surrender after every shot, good or bad. You cannot afford to cloud your mind with what happened on the last shot or how you are going to handle the next hole while you're standing over the shot you're about to play. You must be present, focused on every shot, literally right down to the millisecond. One of the challenges I have with my swing is tempo, which throws off my sequence of movements. There's nothing better than a good-feeling shot. The dopamine hit is so addicting. Rushing and thinking too much is detrimental, whereas being more patient and trusting the process, even in those 1.2 seconds, is where the magic is. If I do all the little things right and have faith in the journey, I will execute. I've proven it to myself. The game might be the best spiritual teacher there is.

***

I specialize in the design and construction of high-end backyard golf complexes utilizing synthetic turf. In 2012 I started Ikes Turf, and for the next five years I fell victim to the mantra of "rise and grind." My life didn't feel like mine. I was chasing something that was outside of me. In the summer of 2017, I was working and staying at my cousin's property, helping with some projects. She was away at the cottage for the weekend, so my wife Terri and our two daughters, Ella and Georgia, came to visit. I decided to work Sunday morning, you know, to "make hay while the sun shines." The plan was to work for a bit in the morning and then chill in the afternoon by the pool. I had been dumping material at the back of the property and I suppose I made one trip too many. As I approached the dump pile, my truck and trailer began to slide on the slight slope and matted down path. SMASH! With no ability to control my truck, it jackknifed into my trailer, crushing the back left bumper and hydraulic pump on the trailer.

I've pushed myself many times before. I've worked through injuries. I've worked unnecessarily long hours. I've had difficult discussions with Terri regarding work-life balance. This was yet another example of trying to do too much. However, this time was different. Inside, I knew I needed to change my patterns and habits. I knew I needed help. On this hot August day, covered in sweat and stress, I made the long, shameful walk back to the house. As I approached Terri in the laneway, she immediately knew something was wrong. I quickly explained what happened and proceeded to have a breakdown on the driveway. I dropped to my knees, bawling my eyes out, yelling and repeating, "I can't do this anymore!" Years of pressure began to release. My efforts to be the best husband, the best father, the best provider, run a successful business—in that moment, every scar, every painful effort, every perceived failure, everything came rushing through. Huddled on the warm pavement, Terri consoled me, feeling helpless and heartbroken in the moment. It didn't help that over our shoulders was Ella watching with concern as her parents cried on the driveway. It was her 6th birthday.

I limped through the rest of the summer only to receive one more gut punch. It most definitely was one more reminder from the Universe to change my ways. I was working on my largest project to date, a 170-yard backyard, par 3 hole. The project was almost complete and we had left for the weekend. I arrived back on a damp October morning and couldn't believe my eyes. A section of the golf green was completely turned over. There had been a massive windstorm over the weekend. Our turf is infilled with sand and by my estimation, we had installed over 5000lbs of sand in the area. Yet it looked like God rolled the turf up like a burrito. I remember feeling numb and having a sense of 'how can one possibly deserve this?' I already knew I needed help—I didn't need the additional, painful reminder.

**

I graduated from the University of Guelph in 2005 with a Diploma in Turf Management. Right out of school, I accepted a dream job as an Assistant Superintendent at a new course being built. Growing up on that golf course is a highlight of my life. For five years, I gave everything I had to that property. It was 2009, and the effect of the U.S. housing crisis was starting to have an impact in Canada. The residential side of the development was suffering and there was a lot of commotion at the club. With weeks left in the season, the chef left, the new GM took another job, the owners fired the head pro—shit was hitting the fan. The owners held a meeting with the turf department to convey that they were happy with our season and there were no concerns about job loss over the winter. With everything going on, I felt like I had dodged a bullet. The next day, the VERY next day, my boss called me into his office as I was punching out. He was laying me off. I remember sucking it up and taking it 'like a man,' the way I thought I was supposed to handle it. As I stood there in my boss's office, while my heart was shattering inside my chest, I didn't have the confidence or the courage to ask what had just happened. I put more effort into making him feel comfortable delivering me the blow than questioning the decision and expressing my devastation.

As I got into my car and left the course, I could feel the emotions brewing, and it wasn't long before I completely unravelled. My dreams felt like they had been stolen from me. Golf was my love. That course was my purpose. It was how I provided for our family . . . I took the long way home to buy time and compose myself. How could I tell my wife? She was a new mother at home with our three-month-old, Ella. It would be over a week before I told her—only after I secured another job. I broke the news while heading to Southern Ontario to see family. We had pulled over in a baseball diamond parking lot so she could feed Ella. I can remember sharing with a grin on my face, partially out of guilt for keeping a secret, but also out of pride that I wasn't going to let her down. Knowing how much that job meant to me and the dreams I had of becoming a golf course superintendent, her heart broke. She wasn't upset that I had lost my job, she was sad because my dreams had been pulled out from underneath me. I learned a tremendous amount during my time at the golf course. Lessons about how to treat people and communication being among the most important. But, the greatest lesson I learned is that I was nothing more than a number on a spreadsheet.

I found work as a window and door contractor, and it was then that I dipped my toes into the world of self-employment. I was trained and I invested in a truck, trailer, and all the necessary tools. I continued with this work for two years, but ultimately it didn't align with me. Something was missing. Golf. I was installing a couple of large patio doors for a customer who was financially very successful. It was around this time that I was looking for a way out of the window and door game, wanting to start a business specializing in synthetic golf greens. This new business was a huge leap of faith because I was leaving something pretty secure and starting something completely new. But I was desperate for change. This man had a beautiful house on the water, a Ford F150 Platinum truck, and a yellow Lamborghini in the garage alongside a boat with wheels! Aside from witnessing his material success, he was a big inspiration and would end up becoming a mentor and partner of mine. I was a sponge when I was around him, the driest sponge you could imagine—I couldn't get enough of his stories about life and business. This man helped reignite my drive to incorporate my passion for golf and my desire to be the husband and father my family deserved. Thus, the beginning of Ikes Turf.

***

I had always been a hard worker. My parents were hard workers. My mother was an administrator with varying offices. I can remember walking into her office of work and witnessing her orchestrating, organizing and responding to anything and everything that came her way. That was her 9-5 on top of managing a busy house of three boys. My dad was a paramedic. His daily grind of shift work saving lives, being underappreciated and underpaid is something I always feel for. I don't know how many lives he would have affected, it's likely countless. With my work ethic derived from my parents, I also believe my instinctual nature to take initiative was because I craved positive reinforcement for my efforts. The grind of seven years of self-employment struggles had piled up and reached a tipping point. I would come to realize I had layers upon layers of unattended trauma. The truth is I had a little boy suffering inside. One who never felt good enough, one who was chasing external validation, and chasing approval from male role models. A young man suffering from societal conditioning and comparison syndrome, I had patterns and habits that were beginning to take a toll on both my mental and physical health. Many times, I felt like I was skating on sand, working with a chip on my shoulder to prove others wrong, to prove I am enough. Working my guts out but not going anywhere.

When I look back, I am so grateful I was paying attention, that I had enough self-awareness to recognize that although I was doing my absolute best, my efforts were harming me. I had no tools to handle the emotional adversity. I would bury them with more work and perspective suggesting I have nothing to complain about. I have a beautiful family, I own a business, I'm "healthy," I live in a great country, I should be eternally grateful. The fact is, I was suffering in so many ways. Suffering from a sense of entitlement, like the Universe owed me. My ego was out of control, constantly highlighting these sentiments; I have worked hard ever since I started working at thirteen years old, I treat people like I want to be treated, I am humble and modest, I am grateful, I have perspective, give me what is mine—I have earned it. Where is it? When will it come? I had been more than patient, and my patience was running out.

After my stressful summer of 2017, in November, I started working with a life coach and facilitator of Brené Brown's Daring Way Program. Brené is a research professor, author, and lecturer who's famous for her research on the topic of shame, vulnerability, and what it means to be courageous. If it wasn't for my coach, I seriously don't know where I would be. Her ability to listen, care, and provide a safe space to share and use her experience and knowledge to help guide me through my awakening is something I shall never take for granted. The Daring Way Program highlights your core values and how they act as pillars in your life. Literally, everything that affects you is in direct correlation to your values, no matter what they are. Your core values are quite honestly a road map for your life. I describe in a few words what this program is like, but it's much more than this, and it requires a lot of hard work. You are going to unpack a lot of shit. And it was so worth it.

Amongst all the success I was having with Ikes Turf, I had held onto so much anger and pain from being laid off in 2009 from the golf course. It took up so much real estate in my head, it's actually embarrassing to admit. I replayed the whole scenario in my mind on repeat. For seven years, seven-fucken-years, I held on to this pain. Until one day, I had worked through it enough and let it go. I invited my old boss into my life. We both still lived in the same town and I was still connected to the golf industry, so seeing him wouldn't be a surprise. But, for seven years, we didn't cross paths. I distinctly remember having those thoughts pass through me and sharing with the Universe, "I am okay if I see him." Wouldn't you know it, days later, I would see him in the printer section at Staples. I found it to be so miraculous. It was a short interaction, but one that helped my healing.

Working with my life coach, I knew I was healing because I was telling a new story. For years I had an automated response when people asked me how I got into Ikes Turf. The story always consisted of my perceived mistreatment at the golf course. My ego just had to tell that part of the story and how I was screwed over. I can still remember my coach praising me. It was in one of our sessions I realized I had finally re-written my story and left out the layoff. It was no longer part of my bio.

***

Have you ever heard the phrase "get out of your own way," but struggle to understand what it means? It means surrender. Surrender to what is, let go of expectations and stop trying to control life. Life will unfold perfectly if you get out of your own way.

The work I was doing on myself was paying off. I was feeling more free and confident in who I was, better than I have ever felt. When it came to Ikes Turf, the seasonality of the business was the main challenge. I had some connections in the U.S. and had been travelling for the previous three winters off and on. The issue was Terri was pretty much a single mom. I needed to find or create something more stable during the winter months. And thus, the birth of The Golf Club. In March 2020, Terri and I opened a new indoor golf facility in our hometown. A beautiful 4200sqft space, boasting five simulators with the best tech, bar, lounge, and of course, a putting green. This project came to fruition lightning fast. From the time the seed was planted, we opened the doors thirteen months later. During that time, I created a business plan, found a space, created the design, organized financing, and completed the construction. Talk about getting out of your own way! After fifteen years with the school board, Terri even resigned from her job to help run the business. We understood it would be hard work, but we finally felt like we were creating something sustainable for our family and something our community would greatly benefit from.

We opened our doors on March 13, 2020, and five days later, we closed them. The pandemic had arrived. From the start of construction leading up to our opening, I worked non-stop for four months. I took only three days off during that time. I was aligned, full of spiritual jet fuel, and I was on a mission. If I'm being honest, when the announcement was made, I was a little relieved that I now got a break, but only because I believed it was temporary. Just two weeks to flatten the curve.

Starting a new business is a unique experience that one might argue you have to be a little crazy to endure because the challenge is so great. Entrepreneurship tests you to your core and acts almost as a catalyst for self-discovery and emotional resilience. All of the ups and downs and the wins and losses are a lot on a good day, so I had no idea what we were in store for when it came to managing the pandemic. Two years of lockdowns, open-close on repeat, twice we had built our bank account up, only to watch it drain again. I'm not sure where we would be today, had it not been for the personal journeys Terri and I had embarked on to strengthen ourselves and recognize our own power. As a small business owner, the roller coaster ride throughout the pandemic is hard to describe, as we became pawns for political theatre. Here is an excerpt from our January 2022 newsletter that we sent to our community:

A business is a living, breathing thing. It has a pulse. It needs to be nourished. On nights when I leave the club after checking on things and the lights are low, it's quiet, and it looks so comfortable and inviting, it feels like we're starving our child. There's no one in the building when it should be busy. That's when feelings of disappointment and anger wash over me. It's disgusting what the government has done to small businesses. We're being starved to death. Some who read this might feel that statement is a little dramatic, but unless you have experienced what we and so many others have gone through, respectfully, you don't get to comment. We just need you to listen. I am simply trying to paint a picture of what the last two years have felt like being considered 'non-essential.'

Navigating and working through the emotions was a lot of hard work and consumed a lot of time. The constant covid conversations with customers became exhausting. I think it was especially tough for Terri and me, (like many who took a similar position) because we never complied. The masks were short-lived. We never once asked a soul for their medical information, nor denied anyone access. There was no way we would take part in segregating the public. We quietly operated our business as usual. In a small way, I think people took comfort in that because we were one of only a few places that provided a sense of normalcy during this shit show.

I think that's why I felt so connected to the trucker convoy. All of my emotions had finally been validated. I remember crying, watching the TV as trucks drove past the large crowds of supporters and watched the unfolding of the next three weeks. I felt like I knew these people. Our family wasn't alone. There were hundreds of thousands of people uniting to support one another. Even though we weren't connected in person, we were connected in spirit.

I became pretty vocal on social media with my views on how small businesses were being mistreated, sharing our story and how irrational decision-making was affecting all businesses. I can't imagine how I would have gotten through the last two years if it wasn't for all the inner work I completed and continued to do. I find it pretty interesting how the Universe has used entrepreneurship as the vehicle for my self-discovery. Through all the ups and downs with Ikes Turf, my stint with windows and doors, and going all out with The Golf Club, it's immeasurable the number of life lessons I have learned being an entrepreneur. I have come to believe that just as much as we are there to make our businesses better, more so, our businesses are there to make us better people. Just like golf, business is a great spiritual teacher. It has prepared me to deal with life that, at times, felt incredibly heavy. I have lived these last two years the most confident and authentic I have ever felt, despite these being some of the most trying times.

Until now, I'm not sure I truly understood or appreciated what all my hard work has achieved. Personal sovereignty. Yes, I get angry, upset, and frustrated, but I'm better equipped to control my reactions to these emotions. The crazy thing about these last two years is the crazier shit gets, the more free I become. Every day I am being tested, and I am constantly going within to bring myself back to the present. The future is yet to arrive and the past has already happened. Centring myself between the past and future allows me to focus, find clarity, and understand that everything is unfolding in perfect order. I work on being in a constant state of surrender to how life is unfolding. The personally dubbed Mind Architect, Peter Crone, has a great quote, "What happened, happened, and it couldn't have happened any other way, because it didn't." The point being is we cause ourselves so much suffering because we believe things should have occurred another way or we want to control how things should go. One of the most powerful realizations is reframing that the mishaps in life are happening for us and not to us. The distinction is so great and a perspective that I consistently use to help ground myself.

When I look back and connect the dots in my life, I'm always amazed. It's easy to see the Universe was conspiring the whole time and continues to do so. My breakdown on the driveway was actually my breakthrough. I could not be and would not be where I am if I hadn't gone through all the valleys. All the problems and challenges are just gifts in disguise. Things are always working out, even when they feel like they are not. I think that's what brings me peace. When times get tough, I understand it's serving a purpose. "This too shall pass," what a great line. I may not like it, and the lows may last longer than I would like, but I know I'll come out of it with clarity.

We are always doing our best from our current level of understanding. I obviously don't know what this life means, but when I am in alignment, nothing feels better. It could be as simple as listening to the birds, a synchronistic moment or accomplishing a very difficult task. For me, that is all the evidence I need that what I am feeling is true, because it feels good. And like Dr. Wayne Dyer says, "Feeling good is feeling God." It's the same word. I currently sit in a state of "I really don't care" because everything is going to unfold exactly the way it's supposed to, because it always has and it always will. I have faith the Universe has my back. I look to take inspired action. As long as my intentions align with my core values, excite me, and to some degree make me nervous—stepping on the other side of fear, then I know I am exactly where I am supposed to be.

JEFF EICHENBERGER

Born in 1983, Jeffrey Alan Eichenberger grew up in Collingwood, Ontario. His natural athleti-
cism provided the ability to excel at youth sports, in particular golf and hockey. The game
of golf would become an integral part of his life and business. His love for the game and the
artistic side of the industry led him to creating his own artificial-golf green company, Ikes
Turf. In 2020 he and his wife, Terri, opened a new indoor golf facility called The Golf Club. TGC
boasts five state-of-the-art simulators, a bar, a menu, and a relaxed, inviting atmosphere.

Jeff's work ethic can be difficult to keep up with, but in recent years he has acquired the
ability to understand when it's time to pump the breaks. Business has been a catalyst for
learning and self-improvement. The lessons he has learned through business are immeasurable, both practically and spiritually. The foundation for his life and business is rooted in
integrity, accountability, and trust. His ability to tap into his feminine energy is a welcomed
strength in the world today. He is empathetic, caring, and understands the skill of being a
good listener. His path to personal freedom was painful at times, but the sovereignty he has
achieved is something he wishes to pass on and support others as they free themselves.

He's not all serious. He can light up a dance floor and his whit can be too much at times.
He loves nothing more than making Terri laugh. They have two daughters, Ella and Georgia.
Becoming a father of two girls has softened his soul, taught him the importance of patience,
while also understanding he may need a male dog in the house soon.

I wouldn't be where I am without my wife, Terri. Words aren't enough. Our girls have been a huge part of my growth as a person and father and I am grateful for their love. I have a great appreciation for all of those who have helped shape me along my journey. I know who they are and they are always with me. And, as Snoop Dogg once said, "I wanna thank me!"

When you struggle, grab your chest &
feel your heart.
What makes your heart beat?
We are connected to infinite energy,
infinite intelligence.
We were all once a single cell that multiplied
into the beautiful beings we are today.
We are born free. We are innately free.
While on Earth our life's purpose is to return to this state.
The Universe makes no mistakes.
Understand life is happening for you, not to you.
Understand you are doing your best.
Understand you are exactly where
you're mean to be.
Faith in these beliefs will make you stronger.
Personal sovereignty is a muscle,
it needs resistance to strengthen.
You are free, we are all free.
Believe it. Stand up for it.
Free yourself & you will free others.

Jeff Eilenburgh

Chapter Eight

THE RISING CLARION

Cassandra Torgerson

October 24, 2019

The sun had set as I gathered the stones collected from the rocky sea beach, a ritual I had done since I was a child. I headed toward the cobblestone streets to seek shelter from the rain that had begun to fall. I had arrived later than I expected but slept on the train from Paris. As I walked the streets of Nice, I allowed my intuition to guide me to the restaurant I would enter. Mid-stride, I stopped and turned to my right, and there it was. A quaint little hole in the wall with maybe ten tables, one of which stretched the length of the room. I shook the rain from my umbrella, placed it in the stand, and took a seat in the middle of the long table. It was a shared dining experience, and it was perfect! The room, full of locals and travellers, quickly filled with conversation. We shared who we were and where we were from. It was my turn. Hearing I was from Canada, a table of local men immediately started to praise Trudeau and commented on the recent election results. They questioned my thoughts on the subject and the room leaned in to hear my opinion. I politely told them that my vote did not go to him and that I had hoped that the next four years would pass quickly, without any major disasters. Just then, the chef came from behind the tiny open kitchen. Overhearing my tone of distaste, he raised my plate high in the air and joked in his thick French accent, "compliments of Mr. Justin Trudeau!" I shot him a sideways glare and smirked back as I took the plate from him, and the room erupted with laughter. There are so many days I think about that trip and that one amazing meal so many miles away. A room filled with strangers that felt like family at that moment. I often wonder if anyone else in that room remembers the conversation and the last statement I made.

April 8, 2021

It has been over a year since the slogan "two weeks to flatten the curve" was uttered. My massage practice was back to full operation after a few lockdowns and hits to the ego. I remembered back to a moment in Grade 4, having to write a dictionary page in detention. Little did I know, that would become a career-defining moment in my life. On the ripped-out dictionary page was the word *entrepreneur*. At that point, I wasn't exactly sure what I was going to be, but I sure liked the idea of working for myself. Even at the ripe old age of ten, the independent, free thinker in me saw the appeal of being an entrepreneur. I knew even then, that no one was going to be my boss or tell me what to do. Yet here I was, rebuilding a year's worth of lost income due to government guidelines.

Massage Therapy wasn't considered an essential service, and I had a really hard time believing that. Clients had called or texted, asking, begging, and pleading with me to work on them throughout the lockdowns. I could hear a tone of desperation ringing in my ears as they sought out an hour of normalcy in the chaos. Even early on, I wondered what kind of sacrifices to our health we had made by complying with these rules.

It was then that I began to notice that so many people would regurgitate the fear propaganda that they heard on the news. For many, the only answer to move through this difficult time was to sign up for the covid vaccine. I wasn't convinced this was our only way out, but I didn't know how to start the conversation or even know who was willing to rationally discuss the alternatives.

One day scrolling through Instagram, I was hit with a story from a fellow Canadian. He was speaking all the words I had been choking on for months. *Enough is enough with just sitting back and not being able to have a conversation about health and wellness and natural immunity when it comes to the virus.* Maybe I wasn't alone after all. I knew there had to be more than just a small handful of people thinking the same way. I envied his courage to speak on all of these topics, while I continued to be mute. After all, how dare we question the science, the lockdowns, the vaccine, or the government and health officials spearheading all of this? We were to follow the government's instructions like diligent little citizens. I knew with every fibre of my being where I stood and what felt off, but speaking up about how wrong this felt still seemed risky to me. I watched his account for weeks, reading both the backlash and praise towards him from his followers. Information warnings began to pop up on his posts. Then he was under a censorship ban, limiting his ability to post, and then one day, his account was simply gone. Just as I had feared, he had been officially cancelled for speaking out. He had been wiped from the social media app, and there was one less voice of reason in a sea of thoughtless compliance.

July 2021

I had looked forward to this family vacation for months. The mountains had always healed my soul. Sitting in the hot tub after dinner one night, a family member asked me the loaded question. Why had I not been vaccinated yet? Not knowing exactly how my answer would be received, I proceeded with caution. The truth was, I just knew I would never get it. Instead, I responded with, "there just wasn't enough information on it yet." The red flags were everywhere for me on this one. The race to get it out on the market between the Big Pharma companies made me feel uneasy. The label read that it was experimental. There were million-dollar prizes handed out in Alberta for those who entered a draw after receiving a dose. Never mind the vax injury stories I was hearing from my clients. A breastfeeding mother whose baby girl started to vaginally bleed after she took the vaccine, miscarriages, numbness and tingling throughout the body, blood clots, facial paralysis, delayed menstruation. *None* of this sounded like anything I was willing to take on. I felt more confident in my body being able to fight off covid than I did in taking this vaccine. The conversation trailed off and it was never really brought up again.

Wow, had this holiday been an eye-opener. It was the first time in years I was subjected to the 6 o'clock news. I couldn't believe what I was hearing. The vile hatred toward those that had chosen not to get vaccinated was seeping from the mouths of each and every person speaking. One morning, a European doctor was being interviewed on an American channel. He remarked that those who have not yet gone to get jabbed were a menace to society, creating all sorts of problems in the healthcare system, and a high-risk carrier for infection to those who have been vaccinated. No wonder my family had questioned my choice. Little did I know that because of the choice I was making, it would be the last time I would see my parents for that year. So, I guess at that point we were officially no longer "in this together."

September 2021

The blame on the unvaccinated for our current situation grew stronger and darker. I would leave work every day and call mom to share the stress of the day. I would tell her how sad and isolating this was making me feel. People I had known for a lifetime had adopted the government rhetoric and began to feel like strangers. Like well-known verses in the bible, the latest catchphrases and wounding words were preached with such conviction.

"It's THEM holding us back from living our lives."

"Throw them all on an island to fend for themselves, they can watch each other die."

"Maybe one of their family members will die, and they will finally wake up and get the vaccine."

"I'm sick of hearing the unvaccinated complain about rights."

"You can bet I treat them as second-class citizens when they come in."

"Well, my kids aren't invited to any more family gatherings until they comply."

These were just some of the statements I heard leaving the mouths of people I thought I knew. I had to ask myself, "had they known my personal choice after uttering those words, would they be able to look me in the eyes again?"

I felt as though I was living a double life, having to hide my choice and in the process, trying not to lose my sense of self or income. I decided to take action and make a sign for my treatment room that read:

"This sacred space has been designed to quiet the mind and help heal the body. Let's use this time together to shut off the chatter of world events. Instead, let's focus on Health, Wellness, and Happiness."

It was now more than ever that I felt that I needed to take care of myself: sunlight, fresh air, movement, meditation, nature, nutrition, and all things self-care. I needed to start making a change for the positive within myself in hopes of seeing it reflected in my outside world.

September 2021 held another dark moment in Canadian history. Trudeau decided to hold another election costing the country over $600 million, to try and gain a majority government. The need for more time to hold power and reign over Canada was so obvious to me. There was complete media bias supporting Trudeau's leadership throughout the country, and the plan to divide Canadians was well on its way. On September 16, he was interviewed and referred to unvaccinated Canadians as "often racist and misogynistic extremists." He then questioned whether the country should even need to "tolerate these people." The votes were in, and Canadians had chosen to keep this tyranny in play. Could the masses not see for themselves what they had done? Or had this vote actually been cast because the majority truly despised the unvaccinated? The goal of conquer and divide amongst the citizens was achieved.

Dark and Darker Days

The end of September meant mandatory vaccination for all healthcare workers as well as federal workers. No travel allowed on planes, trains, or ferries for the unvaccinated was also put in place. We went from free ice cream and lottery tickets to our rights and freedoms being stripped away in a matter of months. Unfortunately, it began to feel like personal choice and freedoms were a thing of the past. And at this point, I couldn't help but wonder, what words were left to hold up the page of the Charter of Rights and Freedoms?

I felt like there was little left to look forward to with the looming vaccine passport on the horizon. A reminder email came through, explaining details of the event I had planned and a refund option if unable to prove vaccine status. Refund it was. I received fewer messages and calls from friends because I was unable to go to dinner, a concert, or a show. There was one particular call that did come through a week before Thanksgiving. Through the receiver, I heard that "I was no longer invited to attend family gatherings until I was vaccinated. Government rules, you know." I could feel my heart break. Their fears and their willingness to comply with ever-changing government rules left me questioning where I belonged. The division felt so deep and raw, leaving an empty crater in my heart. For the first time since this all began, I allowed myself to grieve the loss of the life I had once known. It took four days for the waves of despair to move through me. I spent time walking, journaling, meditating, listening to all kinds of music, and releasing rivers of tears. Then suddenly, I could feel the sadness begin to lift. I missed my freedom and my family, but in the end, there was only one option: *To trust and be true to myself even at the risk of being cancelled.*

January 24, 2022

It was almost 11:00 pm on a Monday night. I should have been crawling in bed but instead, my best friend and I decided to park along a service road on Hwy 2. We were not alone. Scattered along the service road in the middle of a cold winter night were people filled with new-found hope. We stood with flags, flashlights, and proud hearts, waiting for a certain group of truckers to pass by. They had a mission in mind to get all federal mandates dropped and help to regain freedoms in Canada. Now, *this* was something I could get behind. I knew to my very core that this was going to be the start of something big. Cheering as we watched the group drive by, we made plans to go see how many would join the next day.

Early the next morning, we drove in the dark to wait along the Trans-Canada highway. We had arrived early and, like lighters burning in the dark, more glowing headlights gathered along the side of the road to watch. Finally . . . I'd found them . . . these were my people. These were the ones who shared the kindred bond of sovereignty and freedom. Vehicles in the eastbound lane were stretched as far as the eye could see, and as they passed by, the heavy weight that lived in my heart was pulled from me. Tears of joy streamed down my face as happiness and hope flooded through me for the first time in two years. As I watched the last few tail lights crest over the hill, I was able to take my first deep breath in what felt like a lifetime.

January 25, 2022

When the convoy passed through my town, I no longer felt like I was living in survival mode. My protective shell had cracked open. Finding my voice again had been such an empowering feeling. For such a long time, I kept quiet about what I read, researched, and filtered through. There were so many lies built to cover up the truth, and most people continued to believe the mainstream. I try to come from a place of love instead of fear. I believe that the tone and intent behind a message are just as important as the message itself. For two years I had listened, observed, and every so often played devil's advocate with covid conversations. Intuitively, I knew that people were not ready to hear what I had to say. I quickly learned how to dodge the question of "vaxxed or not vaxxed." I had observed that most people just wanted to talk about themselves and their journeys and struggles through this. So, I kept my head about me and asked the key questions to turn the spotlight off me and back to them. It wasn't my normal engagement in conversation, but then again, we were not in normal times. We had been labelled a small fringe minority, but as time passed, the truth came forward, and we weren't that small of a number after all. Being able to find like-minded people and build a community has been such a gift through all of this.

May 3, 2022

The sun begins to set as the smell of jasmine fills the air. Looking across the Adriatic Sea, as I sat sipping on an Aperol Spritz, a wave of gratitude flooded over me. Today I turned forty, and I have planned this trip in my mind for so many years. Each time I visit this beautiful country, I fall more and more in love. The sea breeze cools my sun-kissed skin, and with a shiver, I am suddenly sent back to my body, and the daydream that had carried me to Italy is over. This milestone birthday had been plagued with a different plan. Travel has always been such a major part of my life, and now it seems like such an elusive dream.

When the mask mandates were lifted and rapid testing at airports dropped, clients started asking me when and where my next destination would be. It has always been an easy conversation to talk about my next great adventure. I would start by replying, "I can't leave the country." Most times, they would lift their heads off the table in shock. Wondering what on earth I could possibly have done that would bestow that kind of sentence upon me. I finally revealed the secret I had been holding in after all this time. I had chosen not to get the vaccine and this was the consequence of choosing body autonomy. Most people thought all the mandates were dropped. Even with the suspension of travel mandates, travel is difficult with a fourteen-day quarantine upon return. I'm not shocked at how many people are misinformed on matters that do not directly affect them. After all, we have been bombarded with constantly changing rules and narratives, and who could possibly keep up with it all?

Today

They say freedom comes with a price, and this may be so. I have spent these past years grieving the loss of love, connection, and freedoms that I took for granted before all of this. The fight for freedom is far from over, and the idea of returning to normal has seemed to fade with time. The way things were before the pandemic no longer serves me, anyway.

Growing through this difficult time has allowed me to ground deep into my sovereignty. To find myself so confident in my personal choice that the voice within no longer looks to the outside world for approval. When stripped of personal rights and freedoms, you are left with nothing but yourself. It is then you learn to lean into yourself, to trust yourself, and most importantly, to love yourself on a much deeper level. Would I have arrived at this space without walking through the darkness and pain? Perhaps, in time. But I choose to look at the strength I gained in this chapter of life as an unexpected gift. One that I may not have received or embraced in any other way. Focusing on the here and now and living each moment to the fullest has become my rebellion against the negativity of the past few years. This world has so much beauty and good to offer if we just take the time to acknowledge it. I may not be able to fully explore all far-off lands at the moment, but I have learned to slow down and take note of the wonderful world around me. I know now, with a heart full of love, that better days lie ahead.

CASSANDRA TORGERSON

As a Massage Therapist and small business owner, Cassandra has spent the last twenty years working with clients to achieve relaxation and a deeper connection with their bodies and health. With a passion for helping people, she is always broadening her scope of practice with new treatment modalities in the healing arts. Her philosophy in work and life is to maintain an open mind and a grateful heart.

Residing in Southern Alberta, Cassandra spends most of her free time in nature. A quick escape to the mountains for a breath of fresh air helps to keep her grounded and balanced. Morning walks with her entourage, including her dogs, cats, and Nigerian dwarf goat, have become a welcomed form of daily entertainment. Her love for animals continues to grow as her childhood dream comes true, and her Highland Cattle fold expands each year.

Cassandra's love for creating art was cultivated early on as a child, while she and her grandmother would work on paint by numbers on the kitchen floor. Her artistic interests include interior design, painting, music, photography, and creative writing. Many of her art pieces have been inspired by the places she has been able to travel to.

By staying true to herself, having a huge heart, great work ethic and drive, Cassandra has been able to make many of her dreams become a reality. As her interests continue to expand and challenge her, she finds new ways to continue to bring beauty into her life.

You can follow her journey through this crazy thing called life on Instagram @oxandivy

I cannot begin to express my thanks to Sarah Swain from Trailblazer Media for making this publication a reality. Her courage to speak up, take initiative, and create change is awe-inspiring.

She has brought together this amazing group of authors. I am so honoured to share the pages of this book with you all.

I would like to express my deepest gratitude to the countless number of Canadians who stood up to question "the science" when it was no longer safe to do so.

A special thanks to my friends Natasha and Darcy who have both been an unbelievable source of encouragement through this process. I am forever grateful for their kindness, support, and friendship.

Finally, I would like to acknowledge with gratitude, the continued support and love of my friends, clients, and family.

With a grateful heart
Maryann

Chapter Nine

OVERCOMING A DOUBLE LIFE

Lise Musso

I had been living a double life and didn't realize how exhausting it was. I needed to pick which life would take the lead.

My earliest recollection of being molested as a child was at my grandparent's house. My mom was one of sixteen children, and on Sundays, many of them with their families would gather there after church and have grandma's homemade soup and hot dogs. The kids would play in the basement or outside and the adults would have their discussions at the kitchen table. It was a very big table. A family "friend" would always join the kids and "play" with us. Some were older and wiser and left when he showed up.

Why was I not smart enough?

I was molested by someone else years later and my family does not know who it was. Had I spoken out, lives would have been destroyed, and I wasn't and am still not ready to make that call. My life was already compromised, but calling out this person would have ruined many more.

Why am I protecting this person?

When I was eleven, my dad took a job transfer and we moved to Ottawa for two years. I was sad about leaving my circle of friends, but secretly, I was also happy. I was leaving behind some people I didn't have to see or deal with anymore.

Being a shy girl didn't make it easy to make friends. I had one friend who would call me every morning before school and ask me what I was wearing, and if she didn't like it, she would "ask" me to change. If I didn't comply, she would not talk to me for the day.

Why did I listen to her?

When I would say something she didn't like, she would slap me across the face.

Why did I let her?

We moved back to Winnipeg when I was thirteen. I was so happy to go back home to my circle of friends, whom I missed dearly, and leave behind some people I didn't have to see or deal with anymore.

I'm seeing a pattern here . . .

The next ten years were bumpy but great. One of my abusers passed away and the other I saw a handful of times, but was always on the opposite side of the room. My shyness began to dissipate and I found myself full of life, outgoing, even funny! There was no stopping me. When I was fifteen, I met a boy at school and we eventually started dating. We had a beautiful connection, but something was happening within me. I was so in love, but I became shy, jealous, and introverted again and eventually, we fell apart.

Why did I sabotage this love?

I became somewhat of a loose cannon after that first heartbreak, not knowing where to put my pain. I was drinking a lot, and let's just say I was having "a good time" as I travelled down a promiscuous path, all the while having such a hard time on the inside.

As luck would have it (or the Universe was telling me something ...), an amazing job opportunity fell on my lap that would spark a move to Calgary. I was twenty-three and excited for this new adventure. I was thrilled to leave behind some people I didn't have to see or deal with anymore.

My pattern ...

Luckily I had some friends and family already living there, so my transition was easy enough. In my second year there, I met a man I would eventually marry. He was kind, thoughtful, caring, and loved me. We spent seven wonderful years together before my pattern took hold again and I was off on my own, exploring anew, sparked by an episode of Dancing With The Stars. I had embarked on a series of trips to New York that opened up my eyes to the world of dance and the freedom it brought with it. I was completely enamoured by the industry. The way I felt on the dance floor. The events. The way the bodies ebbed and flowed to the music, and the costumes that adorned them. It pulled me in, and ultimately away from my husband. Out on my own again, I felt free, and my trips to the big city of New York became more frequent, as did the time I spent with my instructor. It felt like I was living in a movie, like the ones you could only wish you were the lead actress being swept off her feet. The chemistry was off the charts and as the depth of this lustrous relationship grew, so did my old ways. I became jealous, bitter, and obsessive until it all ended.

What was wrong with me?

When he started seeing someone else, it was too much for me. I stopped dancing. I went down a rabbit hole of emotions and couldn't figure out how to make sense of them. It was like a tidal wave of suppressed emotions was roaring its way to the surface. A lifetime of running. A lifetime of numbing. A lifetime of pretending I was fine on the inside. Years of believing that I was the problem. This time, I couldn't escape. I couldn't just leave it all behind and start over somewhere new like I usually did. I was debt-ridden from literally dancing my heart away in New York and I had nowhere to go. On October 31, 2009, I wrote a letter on my computer and then tried to end it all with booze, antidepressants, and any other pills I had in the condo. I woke up a couple of days later in a hospital bed, wondering why I was still alive because I sure as hell didn't want to be. Life was just way too hard. I was tired of fighting, of pretending, of acting like life was good. I was tired. I was living a double life and I couldn't do it anymore. They transferred me to a ward in a tiny room with white cement walls and a bed—just like in the movies. My mom and my best friend flew out, and two very good friends of mine from Calgary met with me in a room with a couple of doctors. My mom agreed to supervise me over the next little while so I could be released from the sterile institution and begin my healing journey. My mom took me back home with her, where I stayed for a month and started counselling before returning to Calgary, where I continued my path to recovery.

It took a couple of tries, but I finally found a counsellor that I connected with. It was intense and many times after our sessions, my eyes were so swollen from crying that I couldn't return to work. The pain of rejection, self-abandonment, broken trust, and violation poured from me wherever it could find a way out. Reiki was another form of therapy that helped unearth things within me that I never even knew existed. I was thirty-five years old and on a mission to fix this broken person, once and for all. A year later, and I could finally see life was worth living. I was understanding of my past choices. I was accepting of my actions. I was more forgiving with myself and able to release the shame I had been carrying. With my healed ass in my car, I moved back to Winnipeg on November 11, 2010, to be closer to my family as I learned that leaning into support was actually an act of self-love. On New Year's Eve 2010, I was set up with my future partner. With my therapy fresh, I knew this relationship was different. I was different and very aware. Eleven years later, we're still together and in love, with an amazing nine-year-old boy. For thirty years, my family, friends, and colleagues thought I was a happy-go-lucky, confident, strong, funny, loving individual. Little did they know the agony I was in. I should have received an Oscar for my performance for the double life I lived that no one knew existed.

Then March 2020 arrived and the pandemic kicked off, it was like the last twelve years of therapy and healing disappeared.

We had made it to June and were relieved to feel like things were opening up again. We could gather with a few people, and so we celebrated my son's seventh birthday with family. I told myself life was good, despite the current situation. The problem though, was that conversations always turned to the pandemic. My husband is a strong character and is not afraid to speak his mind. He mentioned some of the books he had been reading that were making him question aspects of the pandemic and was immediately called a conspiracy theorist. The conversation got a bit heated, so I brought out the birthday cake. No better way to diffuse a situation than with cake and a happy birthday song, right? Little did we know that more lockdowns were looming and that tense evening would be the last family gathering we would have for two years.

Things started to get heavy at our house. My husband had been diagnosed with Bell's Palsy, and his doctor had him on some drugs that heavily impacted his mood. My son's hockey season had been cancelled, and I was left to try and explain to a seven-year-old why the NHL players were allowed to play but he wasn't. With each day that passed, my husband was more convinced that something was wrong and that we were dealing with something more nefarious than just a pandemic. I was still trying to avoid it all. I just couldn't grasp or accept how or why our doctors and our government could not have our best interests in mind. It was too much to bear, and I was too busy helping my son navigate remote learning with no extracurricular outlets and working my own full-time job. I could feel myself unravelling. I'd smile and hold my patience each day, and by night, I'd find myself wanting to run and hide, only there was nowhere for me to go.

Somehow, we made it through the school year. It felt like a blur, but I was relieved to welcome in the summer of 2021. It felt like a regular summer. People were enjoying life again and it felt fantastic. I just wanted my normal life back, like so many others. However, things between my husband and I were intensifying. He was trying to point out the elephant in the room that we were on a fast track to government overreach, and I just didn't want to accept it. I wanted to ignore it all and just have my life back, the one I had fought so hard to restore. Often enough, our conversations would get heated and end with me in tears and him frustrated that I couldn't see what he saw. I told him that I needed to figure things out on my own. The thought of him being right terrified me to my core. I needed time and space. Thankfully he respected my wishes and in doing so, he said, "What's right is right and what's wrong is wrong," and that stuck with me.

Why was I having such a hard time dealing with his information? Our doctors and government could not be putting us in danger. Doctors took an oath to protect us. Governments are supposed to work for us. Why didn't I want to see it? Why was my first response to simply trust them? I'm transported back to "Why was I not smart enough when the family 'friend' came to 'play' with me?"

By this time, the vaccine rollout was in full swing. Everywhere you went, everything you listened to was all about getting vaccinated and it's all anyone could seem to talk about. After reading through some of the listed side effects, my husband opted out of the vaccine. His Bell's Palsy was not any better, and as that was actually a potential side effect, he didn't want to be permanently paralyzed on the right side of his face. I was hesitant myself, as I had experienced some severe side effects to medication and flu shots in the past and it felt like it outweighed the risk of what it would allegedly be protecting me from. Remember when I tried to take my life? Suicidal thoughts are a side effect of anti-depressants. Not discounting the healing journey I needed to embark on, the medication I had been on no doubt played a role in the extreme nature of my situation. It also struck me as odd that this vaccine was a new technology called mRNA. New technology for humans, anyway. I understood the dire need for life to return to normal, but I wasn't comfortable with the idea of an experimental vaccine with limited to no understanding of long-term side effects. I simply wasn't comfortable, and so I, too, decided to opt out. Little did I know, this decision would alter our lives in ways we could have never imagined.

Colleagues and friends would ask, "did you get your shot yet?" When I would say no, I would feel the need to further explain my decision in order to restore their sense of comfort. It didn't seem to matter, though, as it was becoming more and more clear that my decision was a deal breaker for many people in my life. I kept thinking to myself, this is my private medical information, and yet it was expected to be disclosed during everyday conversations like the weather. One particular day left me feeling shocked, dismayed, and angry. One of my son's friends came to me and asked me when we were going to get vaccinated because he wasn't allowed to have playdates with my son until we were vaccinated. Here is an eight-year-old asking me my private medical information like it was nothing. All I managed to muster as a response was, "despite what is being said, not everyone can get vaccinated." He looked at me confused.

Why the division? Especially when the science didn't back it up. We knew it didn't stop transmission. We knew it didn't prevent infection. Yet this unwarranted amount of social discord was mounting and left me having to navigate a conversation with a child that wasn't even mine, why a vaccination status shouldn't mean that children can't play together.

By September 2021, we found out our doctor, who was initially not comfortable with my husband getting the vaccine, had conferred with colleagues and had changed his mind. When my husband declined, as his concerns for its safety had not changed, he simply told us we had a moral obligation to get it. *What the . . . ? A moral obligation?* What kind of medical advice was that? Our doctor suddenly did not want to answer any of the questions and concerns we had. Didn't want to? Couldn't? We weren't sure. I was dumbfounded. One thing I knew for sure, though, was that my tinfoil hat-wearing husband had been right. The state of control he had been warning about had finally arrived. Nothing made sense. Nothing added up. But to question any of it landed you in some sort of social prison. It was chilling to finally open my eyes and accept what I had been protecting myself from seeing.

That same month, we found out that we wouldn't be able to watch our son play hockey. Vaccine passports had arrived in our society and exemptions were very few and far between in Manitoba. We knew based on our interaction with our doctor, that even my husband wouldn't qualify. It felt like we were being squeezed out of the world, and now it was impacting our son at an entirely new level. The thought of sending him into the arena alone shattered my heart. *Who would tie his skates?* The worst part is that no one else seemed to care. They were vaccinated and unaffected, and we were told that this was the price to pay for our choice. The ease at which we were being dismissed from the very spaces so near and dear to us sent shockwaves of anger, rage, and heartache through my body. I called my MP, screaming, yelling, and crying. I demanded to see the scientific evidence to support the vaccine mandates. I begged him to look at the science I was looking at. I demanded to know why our choice to not vaccinate was threatening to someone who had. To no avail, the conversation ended much like the one with our doctor. No answers. *How could they do this?*

I found that beneath my anger was a depth of sadness I hadn't known for a very long time. It broke me to pieces telling my son that if he really wanted to play hockey, we wouldn't be able to watch him. "Maman . . . I'll be okay– I really want to play. I'll score some goals for you guys." My heart broke.

***

"I hope you don't get covid and die," was the response on the other end of the phone. I had reached out to family to help my son tie his skates when our friend wasn't able to for one of his tryouts. He had asked me why I wasn't able to go tie them myself, by our choice and our reasons for it didn't matter. "You know what you need to do." I hung up, dropped my phone and sobbed. I was a wreck. The walls were closing in. The days of keeping it all together only to unravel in tears alone at night were all starting to blend together. Family was abandoning us. Friends were disinviting us from games nights, and we couldn't even tie our own son's skates for his hockey games. My healed ass came back to Winnipeg in 2010, to rely on family and friends when the going got tough, but this time when it got tough, they all got going. My entire support system was gone. I was alone.

To compound my already heightened state of distress, our jobs were suddenly on the line. My husband was forced to take a leave of absence without pay. It was a massive blow to our household income. They were coming at us from every angle, it seemed. My job was asking me to attest if I was vaccinated or not. They do not need to know my private medical information but if I didn't comply, I, too, could be put on leave without pay and so I did, stating I was under duress. We needed money in order to live somewhere—I couldn't have my son living on the streets with us. Even the homeless shelters were banishing the unvaccinated. I wanted it to all go away. I was so tired. I was barely keeping it together, even at work. The number of times my poor boss saw me cry. Gone were the days of hiding my heart and pretending I was okay. Canada had become unrecognizable. The sense of safety I once felt had been robbed from me, in a country I loved so dearly. I wanted to run. I wanted to leave. I wanted so badly never to see all the people who had caused me so much pain. A feeling that was all too familiar.

Considerable thought went into leaving the country. My husband and I feared for our son and the world he was growing up in here in Canada. We knew others that had left, knowing the mandates were coming down harder, including the airlines. Eventually, we would be trapped, and the only way to leave would be to escape. Life felt like a movie, only this wasn't fiction. The fact that we were laying the groundwork to start a life somewhere new had really sealed just how grave and hopeless our lives felt. Weighing the pros and cons of staying in Canada or taking a chance in another country felt like an impossible task.

Flight had always been my response. Leave. Flee. Get as far away from the people and situations that caused me pain so I could start over somewhere new. However, the realization hit me that no matter where I went, the pain seemed to find me. What would happen if we uprooted our lives here, only to find more of the same problem in another country? What if we ended up in a worse situation? What if the pain would find me somewhere else?

For the first time in my life, I chose to stay and face it all.

Divinely enough, I saw someone post about some truckers going to Ottawa that same day. *What was this all about?* I was intrigued and followed it with curiosity. Turns out, there was a convoy rolling in from Western Canada, another one coming in from the East, another one coming from Southern Ontario, and they were headed to Ottawa to fight the vaccine mandates and restore our freedoms. We weren't alone! The convoy from the West was reported to be nearly 70kms in length as they made their way into Manitoba. Relief washed over me, and a sense of safety felt restored for the first time in ages. I found myself glued to social media for the days and weeks to come. Watching the videos and posts, I was feeling alive again ... hopeful ... happy. My husband and a friend of his went to Ottawa to show our son what fighting for our freedoms and standing up for what you believe in was about. If our son ever questioned what we did during this pivotal time in our country, we wanted him to know we fought for him and his future. As the weeks went on, my heart was able to regain its strength as thousands across the nation came together in every city, inspired by the events in Ottawa. We weren't the only people who thought we were alone. We had *all* been led to believe we had been the only ones questioning what was happening. The convoy pulled us all out of the darkness and helped us find one another. People from all walks of life united in love in ways I had never seen before.

While it was disheartening and deflating to watch the convoy and peaceful protestors all around the country be smeared by our Government and unjustly dismantled, the pain felt different. It felt bearable. I'm not sure if it was the big-hearted truckers, the love that filled every crack that had been opened with so much division, my years of therapy, knowing I was no longer alone, or knowing I had an eight-year-old son that thought his mom was pretty cool for standing so bravely in what I believed in, but I knew I was going to be okay. I knew we were going to be okay.

I picked a side of my double life. The moment my choice to run away was met with hesitation for the first time, was the day I picked my side. I chose to fight. I chose to speak my truth. I chose to stand tall in my beliefs and if people weren't happy with me, then the burden of the choice to leave could rest with them instead. I picked the side to stop getting slapped in the face, to stop being a victim. I picked the side to be a strong, confident woman who takes care of her family. I picked the side of showing my son to stand up for what he believes in, no matter what others think. I picked the side of living with myself and saying I did everything I could to make sure our rights and freedoms are protected. I picked me. I picked my family. And I wouldn't have it any other way. In the words of my husband, "What's right is right . . . and what's wrong is wrong."

LISE MUSSO

I am a survivor, a mother, a wife, and a friend. I've been through a lot and fought like hell to be where I am today. I love cooking and taking care of people. These past couple of years have taught me that living with integrity is the most important lesson I can teach my son. No matter the cost of family, friends, or employment . . . Living with integrity means I can live with myself, and in the end, that is all that matters. Be kind and be loving . . . the world really needs it right now.

Thank you, Paul and Jean-Luc, for being my rocks when I needed you most. Thank you for your love, support, and understanding. We will always have each other's back because no one else knows what we've been through as a family these past two and a half years.

I have met so many wonderful people in this freedom community. These people have no idea the joy they bring to my life. I'm learning about how to maintain a democracy, how to keep our government accountable, how to homestead, how to make sure that when the system falls apart . . . I won't fall apart.

Thank you for your support!
Writing this chapter was an
incredible journey!

To the freedom community,
may you find solace and love
knowing you are not alone.
To the curious, may you find
the courage to be your authentic
self and use your voice.
To the skeptics, may you
find love and peace in your
journey.

Much Love,
Lisa Musso

Chapter Ten

ALMOST BROKEN

Holly Schefold

I read the text and threw my phone down on the bench in front of the window. I paced back and forth, feeling a surge of overwhelm. Rage rising inside me. I couldn't suppress it. My whole body tensed and I began to panic. I opened my mouth and released the most powerful noise that had ever come out of my five-foot frame. The sheer sound of frustration and agony, simultaneously. It felt like it would never end, that scream just kept coming for what felt like an eternity. And then, it did end. Exhausted and broken, I collapsed into a heap on my couch.

This was not the way it was supposed to happen.

***

As a child, I learned that life was a series of rules. This is how you play the game. Follow the rules, and good things happen. You can veer off the beaten trail to forge your own path in life, but be careful not to venture too far from the norm. You might suffer the pain of having to explain yourself to people who don't understand. Stay within the lines, and things will remain stable. Stability is good. Go to school, get a good job, have a family, retire. At forty years of age, I was supposed to have it together by now. For all intents and purposes, I did. A wonderful marriage, three beautiful children, a stable career. But I grew more and more unhappy, dissatisfied with the pace and repetitiveness of life.

I built a career around serving. Taking care of others and making sure their needs were met. Even when I disagreed with something someone said, I would smile and nod and then internally decide how I truly felt about the subject, although keeping it to myself. Even though I loved my job, I was only half living my life. As if I was living my life like a scoop of vanilla ice cream, knowing that there was a huge bucket of mint chocolate chip and tiger tail just waiting to be devoured, if only I could get out of my own way.

My awakening came unexpectedly. It was not so much a moment of bliss or enlightenment, but more like blunt force trauma. Reaching a breaking point of a life that was so *busy* I barely had time to breathe, let alone do anything other than put one foot in front of the other. I was working two jobs, one full-time and one side hustle that I had started while on maternity leave years before. I knew I was spread thin, but I really enjoyed the sense of purpose and autonomy my second job gave me, and I wasn't ready to let it go. This, on top of keeping a household and parenting three children, was taking its toll. As I lay in bed one night, consumed by tears, I wondered if this was what life was supposed to be like. I thanked God for my husband and children, as they were the only joy in my life. Everything else felt like a chore.

My outside life was reflecting back to me this perpetual state of *busy* everywhere I looked. "Is there more to life than this?" "Is this what we do here? Work, parent, sleep . . . only to get up and repeat it all the next day?" That night in my bed, I heard the voice. Not my voice, but a voice I had heard on previous occasions in the quiet moments. It whispered in my ear, "No, this isn't all there is to life. You haven't got it wrong."

It was a nudge and a foreshadowing of what was to come. Little did I know, the change I was desperately seeking in my life would come in the form of a global pandemic.

Early 2020

Virus. Wuhan. Contagious. "Stay home, stay safe." The messaging was loud and clear. You couldn't drive past a road sign on the highway that wasn't plastered with messaging about what we could do to help fight the virus. I'll admit that in the first weeks, our family was scared. We did all the things. Only one person did the grocery shopping to minimize exposure outside of the home. We wiped down our packages and groceries with disinfecting wipes. We pumped our gas with rubber gloves on. We followed the rules. However, towards the end of March 2020, I had a feeling in my gut that something wasn't right. *Why weren't all the frontline workers getting sick?* I thought to myself one day, standing in line at the grocery store as I watched two cashiers huddle closely at the cash register. *Will we see an uptick in cancers and illnesses down the line with this excessive use of hand sanitizer?* There was a voice emerging from within that was begging me to start asking questions. A voice I'd heard before.

Early 2021

Covid was *the* topic of conversation and all anyone could talk about at work. Case numbers, ICU capacity, deaths. Every piece of information that came into my mind was met by that voice again.

"Is this real?"

"Where are these numbers coming from?"

"Who is calling the shots?"

"Are we really 'All in this together'?"

As I do, I would quietly listen, gathering information. I wouldn't say that I went out of my way to search for alternate news and information but somehow, by way of the Universe, it was finding me. However, the consensus at work was, "When we get a vaccine, we can all get back to normal."

For the last twenty-five years, I have made my health a priority. Working out daily, lifting weights, taking yoga classes, meditating, and eating a fairly healthy diet. I wasn't concerned that I would succumb to covid, should I come down with it. At the same time, I started to hear rumblings of possible side effects of the vaccines. Blood clots and heart problems. I had a medical history that had these things concerning me. Then, the voice that I heard years ago in my bedroom appeared again. I heard it loud and clear "Be patient."

I was relieved to hear that there were doctors who were speaking up and voicing the same concerns that I had. I was equally as crushed when the media and general public swiftly discounted and cancelled them for their scientific point of view.

Watching the vaccine roll out felt like watching a movie. It felt eerily similar to that time I watched society normalize busyness.

As if I was outside of my body, observing. Again, feeling like I was going against the grain and wondering how more people didn't seem to be questioning how things were being handled. I felt very alone, not knowing who I could trust with my questions. The vibe in my workplace was very clear. You didn't question the narrative. I recall being in the staff room one day over lunch in April 2021.

"Has anyone seen the CBC article potentially linking the vaccine to irregular menstrual cycles?" I asked. The women in the room looked at me with a vacant stare. No words were needed. Based on the lack of response from my coworkers, no one was questioning the narrative except for me.

Each day, more and more staff were added to the list of diligent citizens who lined up to get their vaccine. I patiently waited and kept my ears open, wondering if I was alone or was anyone else holding off. A few friends and coworkers opened up and shared that they, too, were waiting for a bit more information. I was relieved. And then, slowly shattered as one by one, they fell. It was easy to pinpoint the moment. As soon as another one decided to get their jab, our chats ended and they were suddenly too busy for conversation, avoiding eye contact. It was subtle yet profound. The feeling, the vibe. As a person who thrived on the validation of others, I started to feel very disconnected from my coworkers. Like a turtle withdrawing his head into his shell, I decided flying low and not saying too much was the way to survive.

I watched on social media while friends also shared their joy in getting their vaccine. Posting selfies mid-poke and attaching a "Let's Get Vaccinated" logo to their photos. I watched couples spend their date night getting vaccinated together and couldn't help but feel that twinge in my gut again. I felt like in years to come, these photos would tell a different story. Suddenly, instead of looking for who *was* posting, I started to pay attention to who *wasn't* posting a photo. Perhaps those were my people.

Even though I had been selective with whom I spoke at work, people were talking, and questioning the narrative was becoming my downfall. We were a company that thrived on the concept of critical thinking, so surely this feeling of being the outcast was all in my head. I couldn't comprehend that asking questions about a private medical decision could potentially cost me my job. But soon, it was clear that I was the pariah and an impending threat at work. Clearly, there wasn't anyone questioning what was happening, except for me. I would hear foreshadowing comments in passing, such as "Maybe this isn't the place for you" or "Everyone is replaceable." I dismissed the red flags that were popping up by choosing to stick my head in the sand, but quietly, they were telling me, "You are not welcome here. You are no longer one of us." My intuition was trying to tell me that what was transpiring in the outside world was not in alignment with who I was. At the time, I thought, "This *is* the place for me. I've been here fourteen years. This job is my whole world."

In April 2021, I received a message from my work. They wanted to meet with me to discuss my "vaccine hesitancy." Although I had never heard that term before, it would quickly become etched into my psyche. I felt my stomach drop. Was I going to lose my job over this? How do I go into this meeting explaining that my hesitancy was based on a *feeling* I had? It felt like my tinfoil hat was starting to show. For weeks on end, I would endure meeting after meeting, in an attempt to show me that I had it all wrong.

I've never struggled with mental health in the past, but I was really starting to question myself. Why did I have to be so headstrong on this? Friends told me that I was being selfish, putting my own health above the collective. Or that the unvaccinated would eventually kill someone someday for their choice. I struggled, hearing these comments from people whom I would consider close friends and colleagues. As a person who lived to serve others, I felt like I was letting them down. Maybe I did have it wrong. I spent many hours questioning my choice. Maybe my children's lives would be so much easier and back to normal if I just got them vaccinated. Their lives had been upended by the mandates as well. No longer able to play sports or go to a movie. My teenage son ate his dinner in a bus shelter one night in the rain while his friends sat inside McDonald's. The irony of needing to show a "health pass" in a fast food restaurant was not lost on me. "Maybe I am the problem. Maybe their lives would be easier if I just wasn't here." These thoughts scared the hell out of me. I knew in my heart I would never go down that path, but it scared me that I was pushed to the point of even thinking about it. In fact, it angered me. That one suicidal thought proved to be a pivotal fork in the road. My instinct was now crystal clear. I wasn't a "No, not now" person regarding taking the vaccine. I was a "No, not ever. And don't touch my kids."

I had lost faith in Public Health because of their lack of transparency and their inconsistent messaging. I had called my family doctor in hopes of getting a medical exemption. I had been told by my employer, if I could secure a medical exemption, my job would be safe. At the beginning of the call, my doctor sounded sympathetic to my needs. My voice quivered as I explained that I would potentially lose my job if I couldn't secure a medical exemption.

Before even opening my file to look at my health history and my concerns linked to the vaccine, she said to me, "I need to tell you that no one is exempt from taking this vaccine."

My heart dropped. "But you haven't looked at my history. Surely I would qualify for an exemption."

It was as if she was reading from a script. This became another moment that would remain in my mind as if there was a master puppeteer pulling the strings. I felt in my heart that she wanted to speak the truth, but she couldn't. The veil was being lifted and the dots were starting to connect.

Our Prime Minister only fueled the divisiveness by calling unvaccinated people racist and misogynistic. Calling on people to exclude their unvaccinated family members from holiday gatherings. The next few months were met with a constant feeling of fear in my stomach. Each day, waking up and not knowing what would come up or what I would have to deal with at work. I had a constant feeling that I needed to run. But where? There was literally nowhere to run to. I heard the voice again. "The only way out is to go in." Meditation became a reprieve from my tumultuous day to day.

By this time, I was hanging on to my job by a thread as I was asked to work from home or only be on site when there was no one else in the building. Slowly, the place I had worked for fourteen years started to feel foreign to me. I considered myself a good employee. In many ways, I was the face of the company, in the sense that I was the first impression that new clients would have when they interacted with us. I would answer emails, texts, and phone calls from my superiors at any hour. Suddenly, there was radio silence. The conversations were still happening, only I was no longer a part of them. I arrived at work one morning at 5:30 am. As I walked through an empty corridor, I heard that voice again. "You won't be here much longer." After fourteen years, I couldn't imagine not being there, but the writing on the wall was starting to come into focus. Eventually, the pain of being part of a community that didn't want me was greater than the thought of leaving.

I could sense my coworker's growing anger and resentment toward me. I couldn't pinpoint whether they were angry at the medical choice I was making, the fact that I was working from home, or because my physical absence left them with a heavier workload. The only communication while I worked from home was curt and to the point, giving me as little information as possible to get the job done. Receiving text messages and emails from them would physically make my heart race as I wondered what I hadn't done or what had been missed, or why they were reaching out to me.

In October 2021, I received the text from my superiors with a deadline. "This isn't working." In two weeks, I would be placed on unpaid leave if I didn't get vaccinated. The final ultimatum. In that moment, I felt a sense of anger but simultaneously breathed a sigh of relief. The days of defending my choice, only to be beaten down and rejected, were over. Never in my life would I allow another person to decide what I should do with my body so they could write me a paycheck. I was angry with myself that I had let it go on so long, clinging to the thread of a position I had left for fear of the unknown. Unpaid leave sounded like a last-ditch effort to push me towards the vaccine. At that point, I asked to be let go from my position.

As painful as it was for me, it was time to jump from the cliff and trust that my body would grow wings. I realized in that moment if I didn't start to create my own dreams and the life I wanted to live, someone else would use me to create theirs. Just like it had been done in the past.

For weeks after, I walked around in disbelief. I would wake up and wonder, did that really happen? Digging deep into myself, I realized it wasn't the termination that upset me the most. As much as I had wanted to look away, I knew that this day was imminent. As if my intuition was saying to me, "We tried to show you the red flags!" I was most upset as to how I had been treated by co-workers, to who I felt I meant more. Some expressed sorrow about my leaving, and others never spoke another word to me again. It felt as if fourteen years of my life were gone in an instant. It felt like a death in some regard. No way to say goodbye. Shortly after my termination, I was bundled up and out for a winter walk with my husband and my dog. As we walked down the main street of town, I glanced into the window of a local restaurant. There, all of my colleagues were celebrating the holiday season with our annual party. The party that I used to plan for them. How ironic that I was literally now an outsider, looking in from the cold street corner.

I decided to accept the situation for what it was. I picked myself up, dusted myself off, and started to pour my heart and soul into doing what I had once loved before covid; teaching children how to cook and bake through classes. I loved the feeling of being in control of my schedule and my finances. I cooked weekly plant-based meals and snacks for local families in order to make ends meet, and was overwhelmed with the love and gratitude that friends, family, and complete strangers poured over me. Not only was I feeling like the creative energy inside of me was being fed, but suddenly my entire life was put into balance. I had time to walk my daughter to school.

I was home when my teens arrived off the bus. I was able to find the time to do all the things I loved during the day (walking, meditation, and the gym), while still having enough time to work on building my new business. Wait! Wasn't this what I had begged for that night in bed so many years ago?

Even through the love of friends and family, there was still an immense feeling of shame that surrounded me and my decision. I felt like an outcast from society and the entire life I had built. I was very careful to whom I shared the reason I had been let go from work, keeping my inner circle very small.

In January 2022, I started to hear rumblings of a convoy. I pulled up social media and couldn't believe what I was reading. Not only were there people pushing back, but there were millions of us all across Canada. For the first time in two years, I felt pure joy and happiness. Watching millions of people come out and cheer the truckers on from the overpasses made me giddy. But then, we were quickly despaired and disheartened by how the mainstream media was portraying the Trucker Convoy. My husband and I decided we needed to see firsthand what was happening and potentially be part of the largest movement in Canadian History.

What we found there filled my heart with joy, love, and hope. It was as if we were in a portal, the real world fading away as we shared the elation of finding others who shared in the sentiment of freedom. Vaccinated or not, everyone there was fighting for all Canadians to be able to choose what was right for their body. People of all ages, races, and backgrounds danced together in the streets on Parliament Hill in -30°C weather, while fireworks blasted overhead.

We would hoist ourselves up to the windows of those big rigs and take the time to talk to the men and women who travelled thousands of miles. One gentleman's eyes welled up as he talked about his two small children that he had left behind in Quebec, whom he hadn't seen for three weeks.

"My wife said, you need to go. You need to go for our children," he said through his thick French accent. We hugged and I thanked him for being there.

"We appreciate you so much," was all I could get out between tears. "Thank you for being here."

He explained they were well taken care of. There was a block mother volunteer who was assigned to each city block of truckers. They would take their laundry home, wash it, and bring it back with food for the tuckers. Each trucker would take turns going home for the night, sleeping in a warm bed, and being treated to breakfast before being returned to Ottawa proper. This is what humanity is all about, I thought. This is how I want to live every day.

Although the final outcome of the convoy was not what we had hoped, my life was forever changed after that cold weekend in Ottawa. I had hope in humanity again, knowing that there were millions of us who were choosing this hill to die on. Others who had felt that inner guidance and chose to listen to it, against all odds. That weekend was the weekend I gained my voice back. I would no longer be silent. The cost of going with the flow and losing my authenticity was so much greater than losing someone who couldn't accept me for who I was.

The moment I decided to step into my power, doors began to open for me. Suddenly, life became a series of synchronicities. What was incredible was that I had lost so many people in my life due to my beliefs, but at the same time, there were new people walking in daily.

And those new friends were showing up for me in ways I could have never imagined. Friends who I had only known for a few months suddenly felt like people I had known my entire life. Our relationships were deep, and there was an understanding and love that was indescribable. They understood what I had been through because they, too, had walked in my shoes.

I was a woman who had been squeezed out of every room before finally giving myself permission to create my own space. That bellowing scream in my living room months earlier was my acknowledgement of it all and a signal that it would no longer have a grip over me. I was done spending time being anyone other than my authentic self.

I knew through the last two years, that my children were watching me. They were absorbing how I was handling this, and they were old enough to understand the consequences of my actions. One night while lying in bed with my eight-year-old, we were discussing how life had changed and all of the silver linings that had come about because of being fired. I asked her if she felt I had made the right choice.

She placed her hand on my heart, "Mama, none of my friend's mommies had to lose their job to show everyone what following your heart really means."

She took my breath away. In that instant, I knew my experience was not in vain. The lesson had landed. No one, no person, no job, nothing in your life is more valuable than staying true to who you are. Your intuition is there to guide and protect you, and your inner compass will always lead you home.

Holly Schefold

Holly Schefold is the owner and founder of Nourish Cooking Co, an online membership that enables children (and their parents) to become independent and self-reliant in the kitchen through plant-based cooking classes. Holly has always been a self-driven entrepreneur at heart. As an AMI-trained Montessorian, Holly worked with children for over twenty years, both in the classroom and in the kitchen before she pivoted to start her own business due to vaccine mandates. Nourish Cooking Co. was born. Holly is passionate about educating children on how empowering it is to make their own foods from scratch.

Holly completed her Precision Nutrition certification and went on to earn her Plant-Based Nutrition certification from the T.Colin Campbell Institute. She's appeared on a few local podcasts and in magazines.

When not in the kitchen, Holly enjoys spending her time with her three children and husband at their cottage near Algonquin Park.

The circumstances surrounding this chapter were life-changing and some of the darkest moments of my life. I am so grateful that these times also brought me closer to the love of my life, Derek, my children, Beckett, Sawyer, and Stella, and also to my parents and sister who never wavered in their support for me. This chapter is for them.

Love Wins ♡

[signature]

Chapter Eleven

GOD, GOVERNMENT, AND CONTROL

Lindsey Stefan

"I feel sick to my stomach, thinking about all the misinformation you've been consuming. I don't even recognize you right now—you've always been so afraid of everything!" said the desperate, horrified voice on the other end of the phone.

"Mom, this is the least scared I have ever been in my entire life. I refuse to live my life in fear anymore." I replied confidently.

The conversation came to a close fairly quickly after that, but that particular exchange lingered in my brain for days. It lingered because of the truth behind what we each said—they were so opposite, but both very true. She was right. I was always a scared little girl, afraid of conflict, afraid of strangers, afraid of disappointing anyone, afraid of making waves, afraid of the future. Afraid of my own existence. So how did I go from that scared little girl to who I am today— someone who boldly stands up for her thoughts and beliefs? I meant what I said. On the cusp of World War III, in a country that has a dictator disguised as an elected Prime Minister, in a world where a pandemic was being used to instill fear in every person alive for two full years—somehow, I have become less afraid than I have ever been. *"How did I get here?"* I asked myself.

After some deep personal reflection, I realized that my path to freedom and fearlessness has really been a process spanning my entire life. My story is one of fear, control, and learning to trust my own inner voice, my own sense of what is right and wrong. The funny thing is that I had to learn this lesson twice.

The first twenty-six years of my life, my freedom was suppressed in so many ways. And in the last five years—I started to fight back. I had a very religious upbringing, and while that is not a bad thing in itself, the religion I was raised in was extremely strict—some have gone as far as to call it a cult. Whatever you want to call it—it suppressed my freedoms. I was not free to ask questions, I was not free to be friends with anyone outside the religion, I was not allowed to pursue post-secondary education, I was not even allowed to watch Disney movies. Don't get me wrong, my parents loved me and provided for me, and I have nothing against them for raising me this way. They did what they thought was best, and didn't mean for it to affect me like it did. But I used to have nightmares about God killing me, and I lived in constant fear of Him executing judgment on me at the end. Living in that fear of making one wrong step was stifling and depressing. It left me with a hole in my soul—I always knew there was more to life for me, I knew there were answers to my questions out there, I knew that I wanted to experience freedom and to choose what freedom meant for me. I knew all of that in my heart, but I suppressed those thoughts. I was too afraid. I knew that if I left the religion, it would mean losing my family and everyone I knew and loved. It would mean starting over, in every sense of the word—I'd seen it happen to people I loved who had left before—including my dad. So, I stayed and felt the gaping hole caused by fear in my soul get bigger and bigger, and let the religion control me, my thoughts, and my feelings.

Finally, in 2016, at twenty-six years old, I let that gaping hole get so big that I was forced to make a decision. I explored what my options were in my own mind. I could live in fear of God killing me, or I could take matters into my own hands. Logically, the answer was to kill myself—I could take the fear of God and death away by taking control and taking matters into my own hands. But instead, by some miracle, despite an entire province separating us, my dad saw what a mess I was. He saved me. I remember how much courage I had to build up to finally have the conversation, and tell someone what was going on in my head.

"Dad, why did you leave?"

He took a deep breath and exhaled slowly. I knew he hated it when I asked these questions. I'd asked him before, but I don't think anything could prepare him for what I said next—before he could answer.

"I'm asking because I want to leave. I can't do it anymore, and I'm scared of what will come next. How do I do it?" I asked through a shaky breath—fighting back tears, hearing the words finally spoken out loud.

This was the most open and vulnerable conversation I'd had about my faith, or lack thereof, in a long time. He told me his reasons and said:

"You aren't in a state to be making big decisions right now. You're depressed. Let's get you better, and then if you still want to leave, I will support you, and we can figure it out together then."

He'd given me the permission I needed to heal and to leave my old way of life behind. I was reassured that I had at least one person in my corner when it came time to make the final decision. He made me move home to Calgary and helped me get my mental health back on track. I still don't even know how he knew to come visit me for a few days, but I thank the Universe daily that he pulled me out of that dark place and gave me the strength I needed to make the hardest step of my life—which I can now look back and identify as the first step on my path to sovereignty. A step I don't know if I ever would have taken on my own.

Once I took a step back from letting my thoughts and actions be controlled by fear and propaganda, I could stop and listen to my own voice. The voice that was telling me there was more to life, more to the world as I knew it, more to *me*. I remember starting to make choices that I had never been able to make before, flexing that freedom muscle repeatedly, getting a feel for it. I got my nose pierced, I got a tattoo, I went to a club for the first time, I listened to the music I wanted to listen to without guilt. I got to know who I truly was, what I liked and disliked. I observed who I was and how I felt in different situations. I got to know myself—who I really was at my core, without the expectations and limitations placed on me. It was very awkward at first—just like the first time you went to the gym and tried a new workout. But once I got a taste of that freedom, I never looked back. I started living my life how I wanted to, showing up authentically as myself, and have loved every second.

**

By 2020, I had completed my post-secondary education, made some amazing career moves, married the love of my life, and healed some very big emotional wounds—or so I thought. I thought I was living as freely and authentically as I ever would. I was finally happy. Then covid hit the world like a ton of bricks, and it was as if all of the work I had done to relieve myself of living in a constant state of fear was unravelling by the minute. My world crumbled. I returned to my life of fear and control. I stayed inside, I washed my hands, and I wore my mask, reverting to that scared little girl as if the last five years of self-discovery and healing hadn't happened. I let the government become my new god. A god that ruled through fear and a constant flow of propaganda—controlling its subjects in the name of safety and survival for all.

I found out in early September 2020, that there was a tiny little being growing inside of me. My husband and I were absolutely thrilled. And completely terrified. I don't even mean the normal fear that all new parents face when you find out that your body is housing another human being to be brought into this world. I mean absolute sheer terror at bringing a tiny life into a pandemic. It was horrifying. I lived those nine months in fear of getting sick. I lived in fear of my co-workers who got too close to me without a mask. I suffered sitting in a warm room with a mask on, on the verge of passing out (anyone who has ever been pregnant knows that breathing is not easy, even without a mask!). I saw posts on social media about babies who were born to moms who had covid and were so ill, or moms who went into premature labour because of covid. I lived in fear of losing my baby, but also in fear of him coming into this uncertain world. The fear absolutely consumed me. I now look back and realize how much I was robbed of my joy, for the second time in my life.

By this time, I was slowly starting to wake up to what was going on in the world. Vaccines were rolling out, and I was told they were safe for pregnant and breastfeeding moms. This left a heavy feeling in the pit of my stomach. Many family members urged me to get it so the antibodies could be passed on to my unborn son. But when I looked online, I could see that the information across Canada wasn't even consistent. Some provinces started by having pregnant women sign a waiver, some stated that pregnant women shouldn't get it, while others (mine) pushed pregnant women to the top of the list and let pregnant women get them along with the elderly and other high-risk populations. How was I supposed to trust something that the leading doctors of my own country couldn't even unite their opinions on? It just didn't sit right, so I refused, telling people I would reconsider when he was born, and then again when he stopped breastfeeding. I am grateful every single day that I didn't let myself be bullied into doing something with even the slightest chance of harming my baby. I am so glad that my intuition, even at that early stage, didn't allow me to inject my body and my baby with experimental gene therapy. And honestly, I am so glad that I had my sweet boy with me to protect me. Without my mama bear instincts to protect him, maybe I would have gotten it for myself. I don't know. But I do know that without him, my story would be very different.

In May 2021, my beautiful baby boy was born, and it was exactly like everyone describes—the instant love you feel for your baby is like nothing I've ever felt before. But again, I was robbed of the normal experience—my first photos with him, and our first photos as a family of three, have my husband and I masked. At this point, I was still in the early stages of realizing what was going on in the world. I knew vaccine mandates didn't sit right in my gut, but I didn't think much of masks and lockdowns—we needed to stay safe, right? I shudder now at the thought of how many people held my son while wearing a mask—the expressions on people's faces that he missed out on, the speech development that so many "covid babies" are struggling with. A whole generation that is stunted because of their early days of being subjected to such a damaging environment.

As time went on and so did the fear-ridden pandemic, my own fears that had resurfaced in my life and robbed me of my power turned into full-blown postpartum anxiety. My husband would find me more than once in a sobbing mess on the floor.

"How could we be so selfish? Why would we bring him into this fucked up world?"

"We're going to do our best and be good parents and protect him as best we can, Lindsey. He'll be okay."

"I love him so much, though; how could I do this to him? I wish we didn't have him. Either God is going to kill him soon, or he's going to grow up in a world of fear, sick people, and evil. What does his future really look like? What have we done?"

I thought I'd moved past this, but clearly, my deep-seated fears had just been suppressed for so long that I thought they were gone. Having a baby and being responsible for a life other than my own brought it all back with a thunderous vengeance. It was my job as his mom to protect him and care for him—but how was I supposed to protect him against the wrath of God? I felt like I had already failed him just by bringing him into this world, into a world I was so afraid of myself. People around me thought I deserved to die, that my baby deserved to die because I was unvaccinated. How much worse were things going to get? How long until they came to get me and take my baby away to put me in a quarantine camp? I felt completely hopeless.

With the help of my doctor, I was referred to an amazing therapist who helped me work through my guilt, intrusive thoughts, and fear. The more I examined and dove into my belief system and my past, the more I started to see parallels between the fear the governments were using and the fear that I grew up with. I'd been taught my whole life that we should segregate those who believe differently than us. That their actions could somehow make me "sick" spiritually, that even having a conversation with someone who wasn't of the same religion would weaken me, and even the slightest question or shadow of a doubt could make God abandon me altogether. Now here I was again, seeing the masses being encouraged to shun those who weren't vaccinated, those who asked questions, those who contradicted the "science." The similarities were undeniable! It was sobering and heart-breaking to me that I had been duped again. How could I have let this happen? I felt so alone. I knew only two other people who felt the same way as me. So, I started seeking out fellow unvaxxed people on social media, and I also found some really wonderful activists that had left the religion. They were all saying the same thing! Every YouTube video I watched, every Instagram post I'd see from one or the other, I drew the parallel between the activism of the ex-religion to the freedom fighting from the government. My favourite quote that deeply resonates with both is, *"The truth does not mind being questioned. A lie does not like being challenged."* I was waking up hard and fast to both. I was watching the walls of the world I thought I knew crumble around me in every way. I felt liberated and free and absolutely terrified, all at once. I finally knew that I wasn't crazy. I finally saw the world for what it was—our leaders were puppets, who didn't give a fuck about my well-being, and money controlled so much more than I thought. But there were so many beautiful people in the world like me—people who wanted to break free from the systems, people who were good and wanted to live freely. I finally felt hope for the future again. Waking up to the world around you being a total lie is earth-shattering, as many of us know, but it is so beautiful on the other side.

I now feel like I am living in two different worlds. The world where I follow preppers and homesteaders on social media, and I have conversations with my awake friends about what items we should have on hand to be able to barter with after the impending financial/societal collapse that we all see coming. But then there's the other world. The world where I go to the mall or the grocery store, and it's like nothing is happening. Like everything is completely normal. Like I'm not waiting for society to collapse at any moment and need to pack up my car with my prep gear and get the heck out. But the beauty of it is that I am not afraid. Knowledge is power, right? My power and refusal to be ruled by fear comes from the knowledge that I have that many others choose not to see. I have a backup plan—a plan to escape from the system. I couldn't possibly fight an all-powerful God, but I *can* fight the system. I can prep, save, and study homesteading and survival. I can learn politics, take part in protests, and write to my MPs. I can regain some sense of control and feel like I am fighting for the cause. Why would I be afraid now when I am in a better position to fight back than most people around me?

I lived in fear of a cruel God waiting to kill me. I lived in fear of healthy people around me. That fear that I used to live with was put there by people who wanted to control me. And while I do still feel afraid at times for my son's future and for the future of the world as we know it, I feel confident that I am a part of a community of people who have our eyes open and are prepared to take on what the world wants to throw at us. We prepare, we think critically, we are self-sustainable. Most importantly, we love each other and trust in the future. Together and apart, we are sovereign, and for the first time in my life, I am sovereign.

LINDSEY STEFAN

Lindsey currently lives in Calgary, AB, with her husband, her one-year-old son, and her two fur kids—a tabby cat named Lulu and a Jack Russell Terrier, Jovie. When she isn't busy being a mom and a wife, she enjoys doing dog sports with Jovie, going for walks with her family, being in the kitchen baking delicious treats, and dreaming of her future homestead life. Friends describe her as determined, caring, strong-willed, and ambitious; someone who can be counted on in times of need. She is always working on some new, completely outrageous goal or project.

The first acknowledgement must go to my dad, Wayne. He is the person I care most about in this world about what he thinks of me, which constantly challenges me to be better. Thank you for believing in me and constantly supporting me in everything I do, Dad. I love you! Thank you to my wonderful husband, Garret, who supports me in all my crazy dreams and goals and does everything he can to help me achieve them. He is always there for me and has absolute confidence in me and my abilities—even when I have no confidence in myself. Thank you for being my best friend and life partner. Jallaina and Jana, thank you for being my friends and fellow freedom fighters, I love you more than you can possibly know. Mom, thank you for making me who I am—you and I do not see eye to eye on things all too often these days, but it challenges me to examine my beliefs and perception of the world and prove them to myself, and for that, I am grateful. Sarah, Meags, and the whole Trailblazer team—thank you for believing in me and letting me share my story. Finally, Milo, thank you. Thank you for choosing me to be your mama. Thank you for being my reason to fight for freedom, for being my reason not to be afraid, and for proving me wrong at every opportunity. I love you so much, and I will work every day to leave this world a better place for you and for your future.

Together + Apart,
We are sovereign.

Chapter Twelve

LIFE IS GOOD

Courtney Hobbs

The sign read, "For accessibility options use other entrance." After an hour's drive, a parking spot a kilometre away, and no actual idea where the other entrance was, I picked up my nine-month-old, stroller and all, and proceeded down the stairs. The damp, metal smell of the subway filled my nose. In the distance, we could hear the rumble of the trains. Marley was wide-eyed. I bought tokens and we entered the platform. I sat Marley beside me while I folded the stroller and took a breath.

"We're here baby," I said. "Our first Toronto adventure!"

She smiled and then jumped as the train rushed in, filling the quiet station with a squeal. I slung the stroller on my back, picked Marley up, and we boarded the train. While we travelled, I told her about how mommy used to live in Toronto. I explained that the trains would take me on all kinds of adventures around the city. I told her this would not be her last subway ride because we were going to have all kinds of trips together and experience all this city and the world had to offer.

"Ding, Ding, Ding." The chimes sounded, the voice instructed us, and we got off to make our southbound transfer. We headed out the doors and down the escalator. I could see her at the bottom. Her bags surrounded her. She was dirty and had missing teeth. She was probably going to ask me for money. I could feel it. And no one else was around. I did not want to make eye contact. Sweat was dripping down my back. I was in a hurry and mid-trip. But Marley smiled. The connection was made.

"How cute are you?" she exclaimed. "How old is she?"

"Nine months," I replied, half smiling, half trying to get away.

"Where are you headed?" she asked.

"To see Santa at the Eaton Centre. We are meeting our friends there," I explained.

"Well, that sounds like fun. You two enjoy your day."

"Thanks, you too!" I said and hurried away.

It was that brief. No asking for money. No long, drawn out chit chat. It was a smile, a brief connection, and a moment I'll never forget. Not for anything other than the reminder from my nine-month-old, that a smile can go a long way. A conversation, even a short one, can stick with you and is worth it. Human connection is really what it's all about.

On our trip home, as the subway screeched and skidded along the track, I replayed the day in my head while Marley slept in my arms. At that moment, I was so grateful for this, our first of many adventures. I sat there dreaming of the exploring we would do and the connections to people and places we were going to make.

I looked at her little face and thought, life is good.

The last time I had a true 'life is good' moment was the day before my husband's father, Sam, suffered a brain aneurysm. It was the holiday Monday of Thanksgiving, Ben and I were engaged to be married, I had just run my first 5K, and I was the healthiest I had been in a long time. I remember hugging my future father-in-law and him saying, "I love you." I loved how he was always so open with his feelings. He and I were similar in that way and we always got along well. I loved him too, and always reciprocated the sentiment. This day was no different. And I was so grateful I did, when not forty-eight hours later, we were racing to the hospital, watching them drill into his head and then sending him by air to another hospital better able to handle his life-threatening state.

My father-in-law succumbed to his brain aneurysm and all the complications that came with it about six months after that October event. It was some of the most painful months for our family. It set in motion for me an understanding of how precious life is. How every moment is important. Yet, it also left me feeling afraid to feel too happy again. I was afraid to feel the goodness of life for fear it would bring another tragic event.

But that day in the subway station, two years later, I allowed myself to fully feel the joy again. A lot had happened over those years, and I was living a life I was proud of. I had left my teaching job, started my own wellness business, and had a healthy and happy baby girl. Life *was* good and I wanted to feel that despite what might happen next.

Before Sam's death, I had spent a lot of my life playing by the rules. Following a path that was honourable and acceptable. I had three degrees, a secure job as a teacher, a pension, a mortgage, and a loving partner. But on my 30th birthday, when my parents generously paid off my student loan, I started to become unravelled. I had been keeping myself alive to pay off that loan. I was depressed, burnt out, and lost. I wanted to die, but I did not want to leave Ben or my parents, the people I loved most, with the burden of having to pay that debt. So, I kept working my two jobs, going above and beyond in all my roles, and ignoring the blackout exhaustion I was experiencing. I ignored my racing heart and constant anxiety. I kept putting one foot in front of the other. I kept showing up. I kept suppressing my pain because I had a loan to pay off.

The day after my birthday, I arrived at work with frizzy curls, translucent skin and wearing an oversized sweater that barely hid my dishevelled appearance. I walked through the school halls, wondering what I was even doing at work. By lunch, I was numb. Two caring coworkers asked if I was okay, and it all spilled out of me.

"My parents paid off my student loan for my birthday, and now I don't know why I should keep living," I said as I started weeping.

We all sat in silence for a moment, and then they both took action. I am grateful every day to them for taking my words seriously.

"I'm going to tell the office you need coverage for your afternoon classes," one said as she left the room.

The other grabbed a pen and paper and started writing down my next steps.

"Call your doctor, call the union rep, call the Employee Assistance Program," she read out to me. "You need some time off to help yourself."

The rest is blurry to me. But I left the school that afternoon and didn't return for five months. Over those months, I learned that the weight of that loan made me feel stuck. Stuck paying back a loan I had from an education I needed for a job I didn't want. Through this realization, I became more alive than I had ever been as I started to explore other ways of living. I saw the world and my place in it differently than I had before. Despite friends and family thinking I was crazy to leave a secure pension and a job I had worked hard for, I knew my life depended on me carving out my own path. After Marley was born, I started my wellness business and never returned to teaching.

By the time my second daughter arrived on a snowy night at the beginning of 2020, I felt like life couldn't get any better. My business was thriving, my children were thriving, I was thriving. I was living the most authentic version of my life I had ever experienced, and life was good!

Fast forward three months and I was calling my mom, crying into the phone, "Can you come over? My milk ducts are clogged again, I am in so much pain, I can hardly do anything for Marley, and I just need to have a shower. I don't want to put you at risk though, but we haven't been anywhere or seen anyone and we feel fine, but it's up to you."

"I'm fine with it and so is your dad, but what will your neighbours think?" She asked.

"Well, Ben and I were thinking you could park in the garage and then come around back, shower and change your clothes, and then come upstairs. And then maybe stay over for a night or two?" I suggested.

My mom, who wanted nothing more than to be a grandma, responded with a quick, "Perfect, I'll see you tomorrow."

I exhaled a sigh of relief. Three weeks into this pandemic and I could feel my mental health slipping. A three-month-old night owl, a wild and witty two-year-old, a string of clogged milk ducts, and no capacity to pivot my business, meant I felt overwhelmed, exhausted, and lost. I needed support, but almost everyone that helped me stay healthy was locked away from me. Mix in knowing the only covid patient in all of our circles was currently hooked up to a respirator fighting for his life, made this all very real. So, I was scared to break the rules. But my mental health, my baby's health, and our household health were proving to be larger issues than the virus, and I was willing to take the risk.

After my mom's stay, my husband's mom came, and then my mom came back again. The help was life-saving. But on Zoom calls with friends, I would hide our rule-breaking. I would nod sympathetically while others complained about missing their support networks, secretly knowing mine was downstairs rocking my baby to sleep.

By the summer, some restrictions were lifted and my world started opening back up. I was able to run my business again, but it wasn't the same. The virus chat became monotonous fast. I didn't want to talk about how to wash my hands, what sanitizers were best, or the latest mask trends. Yes, I wanted everyone to be safe and healthy, but I refused to live in fear. I had done that before. Maybe not from a virus, but I lived in fear of myself and my anxious mind every day for a long time, and I did not want to do that again.

I worked hard to change the conversations. I worked hard to lead by example. I stopped listening to the news. I shared how the only person I had known to have covid had survived. I refused to download the contact tracing app so I wasn't on edge with every outing I made. And I grounded myself in what I was able to control.

* * *

The cold weather brought the return of lockdowns. We were so fortunate, though. I pivoted my business online this time, our daycare was running, and I had some friends and family who were willing to gather quietly to celebrate life's milestones. These opportunities to keep connected brought me joy and kept me going.

When the covid vaccine started rolling out in early 2021, I didn't give it much thought. Sure, the post-apocalyptic obsessed side of me casually joked about how fast it had rolled out and questioned people on if they had ever seen *I Am Legend* or *The Walking Dead*. But, beyond that, I was indifferent. I felt I did not need to be first in line to get it. I was a healthy thirty-five-year-old who had only ever gotten the flu shot once but had always survived flu season. So, I decided to wait. Other people needed it more than I did. And as I watched others celebrate their jab, I genuinely felt happy for them. I felt the less people were living in fear, the better we would all be and the sooner we could get back to normal.

But when you're indifferent to something that wants you to have an opinion about it, you start to see differences very quickly. People start to confide in you. They explain their infertility battles and how they don't have enough information to know what to do. Or they are pregnant and question tragedies like thalidomide. Or share the research they have done that concerns them around unknown side-effects. I couldn't help but start to consciously question what was happening. But almost instantly, I learned that that was not allowed in most of my circles. So, I censored everything I said to the point of becoming silent.

I gradually pulled away from my business. I showed up but my heart wasn't in it. I no longer felt like I could be my authentic self. I no longer felt like I could give my honest opinion or advice to wellness seekers. The life I had been creating for the last couple of years was slowly fading away from me, and I could feel my mental health fading with it.

I attended a virtual business event in May 2021, and I listened to people preach about entrepreneurship. I heard them sharing ways to make more money, build your business, and set goals—all things I would have cheered on previously, but I felt so lost. I had no idea what my next goal would be. I felt like I lost the ability to dream. I couldn't recognize the world we were living in. Where were the subway adventures I once had with Marley? Where was the business I traded in my safe job for? At one point, we wrote ourselves a letter to be delivered back to us at a later date. My letter started like this: *So, you'll either be dead or happy when you get this back.*

I did not want to feel the way that I was. I had put in years of work up until this point to stay strong and healthy, but without community, without a clear vision of the future, and without the ability to be my truest self, I wasn't sure I wanted to be around. I kept questioning, what was the point?

***

One July night, I found myself on my couch, computer in my lap, sobbing. Like, can't catch your breath, spinning out of your head, sobbing.

I stared at the blinking cursor. I had just written:

"Marley, you made my dreams come true. You are so beautiful and amazing."

I pictured her through my tears. Her long blonde ringlets, her bright blue eyes, her little three-year-old hands. I heard her giggle, saw her love, and felt her joy. But just as clearly, I saw her pain, confusion, and terror at learning her mother was gone. And all that she had was this letter, trying to tell her a lifetime of advice and sum up an eternity of love. It hurt my heart in a way I had never experienced pain before.

I stared at the screen, trying to figure out how I could explain to her the hate and anger I felt for the world and myself, but also how she should live her life to its fullest. I felt like such a hypocrite. I picked up my phone and started scrolling through my photos.

I saw our smiles while we baked muffins and did family workouts. I saw our winter hikes, our dance parties, and my daughter's joyful faces. I couldn't catch my breath. What was I doing? Life was good. Sure, our adventures looked different and were closer to home, and my business wasn't thriving the same, but we still had each other.

What followed that night was confiding in my closest friend about my plans to take my life. She helped me find a therapist who supported me in reaching out to my doctor, and eventually, I was diagnosed with ADHD and I started taking medication. This event coincided with my turn to get the Covid-19 vaccine. As someone who was hesitant to take much of anything prescribed and who had been consciously questioning this jab, I decided I would wait and take on one side effect at a time. I wanted to see how my new ADHD medication settled in my system, and then I would decide on the jab.

This decision did not come without judgment, ridicule, and consequences. People said they understood but promptly followed up with my being uninvited from the party/dinner/event because I was dangerous to others.

By September 22, 2021, the first day of the mandates restricting people like me from doing pretty much anything, I was two weeks into my meds. By this point, Ben had received his two doses to play hockey. He was craving exercise and social outlets. He was also getting pressure from work, which was important for our family.

The next few months were the darkest I've ever experienced. The harshness and cruel divisiveness were straight out of stories from the history books. I took strength from these stories of people who were now celebrated but hated for their choices in their lifetime. I cherished the small things like being able to order take-out or watch movies online. And I valued the bigger things like Marley still being able to attend her dance lessons and Ben being able to take her.

But the biggest moment of clarity came in November after a terrifying middle-of-the-night event.

I was tending to Clarke, our youngest, who was vomiting. Marley had woken up and I needed some help. I woke Ben to assist, and not two minutes after him getting up, I heard the thud of my six-foot-tall husband hitting the floor, followed by my three-year-old screaming "daddy" over and over again. I ran to her room covered in vomit with Clarke in my arms to see his pale, lifeless body lying on the floor, stiff and unresponsive.

"Ben!" I screamed, tapping the floor by his head like I was taught in my CPR classes. I ran to get my phone and dialled 911 as I raced back to him. While it rang, he came to. In a panic, I hung up. He was dazed and tried to explain that he wasn't feeling well. He walked hunched over to the washroom.

"You're okay, mommy. You did really good," Marley encouraged, as she put her little hand on my shoulder and stared at me with her bravest face. And then I heard it. Another thud. I went running.

Once again, his pale body lay motionless on the floor. But this time there was blood. He hit his head on the way down, and his lifeless, pale body was twisted in a position you only make if you're dead. I dialled 911 again. As calmly and clearly as I could, I explained that my husband had collapsed for the second time. He was unresponsive and bleeding from his head. I gave her my address, and she said help was on the way.

Then she asked how old he was. All time stood still.

"He's thirty-six," I responded, but my mouth was dry and my voice had left me.

"How old is he?" she asked again.

"He's thirty-six," I tried to say again, but she didn't hear. I tried one more time, and finally, I shouted it into the phone.

"Okay," she said. Then she instructed me to turn on the lights, open the door, and put my mask on. The firefighters arrived minutes after, followed by EMS. With Clarke in my arms and Marley attached to my leg, I answered their questions and directed them to where he was.

He was awake when they carried him down the stairs and put him on the stretcher. I could talk to him before he left in the ambulance. I told him I was trying to get a hold of his mom or brother to meet him at the hospital, but they weren't answering. I said my parents were on their way to watch the girls, and I would come then to be with him if I could. I kissed his forehead and went back inside.

My neighbour, a doctor who was always awake, saw the commotion at our house and messaged to see if she could help. I explained as best I could over text what happened, and she offered to sit with the girls or drive me to the hospital once my parents arrived.

"I would appreciate a ride to the hospital" I started typing and then froze. Was I even allowed in the hospital? I tried calling his mom and brother again before I wrote her back. Still no answer.

"I would appreciate a ride to the hospital . . . but I'm not double vaccinated, so I don't know if I'll be allowed in. Would you mind waiting once we are there to see if they let me in?" I had nothing to lose at this point. I wasn't letting my husband be alone at the hospital. She could judge me all she wanted.

"I have good masks," she wrote back. "And the rule just started yesterday, I'm sure they will bend it for you. I don't mind waiting to see".

"Thank you," I replied

I was greeted by a volunteer upon entering the hospital. I told her my husband was just brought in. "You can scan here," she instructed.

"I'm not vaccinated," I replied.

"Just scan here, and we'll see," she insisted.

"I don't have anything to scan, I'm not vaccinated," I repeated.

From behind a plexiglass-covered desk, I heard a nurse ask, "Here for Ben?"

"Yes," I said, turning and looking.

"I'll take her back," he said, half to me and half to the volunteer.

The volunteer gave me a visitor sticker and I followed the nurse toward the ER beds. As we walked, he said under his breath, "the rules are stupid." I kept following.

"Thank you," I said, locking eyes with him as he opened the curtain to where Ben was.

Once the tests were run and the only explanation of cause was dehydration, we were told we could go home.

At this point, my mother-in-law was at our house with my parents.

The girls were asleep and they told us to go to bed, too. I couldn't sleep. I felt uneasy with the lack of explanation we were given. I reached out to a few close and trusted friends, explaining what had happened. One sent me a link to a video of dozens of athletes collapsing just like Ben did. I sobbed.

I may not be a doctor or scientist, but my degrees proved to me that I could do research and draw a conclusion. I spent hours upon hours reading, listening to, and consuming all the information I could find. I became obsessed with the banned, blocked, and cancelled information. My indifference to the vaccine soon became a solid choice. The hatred I heard from people felt clear to me when they said,

"Those people deserve to die."

"They should be locked up."

"Schools should be segregated between vaccinated and unvaccinated."

"They are selfish assholes."

And the questioning about freedoms I no longer had, suddenly didn't carry the weight they used to.

"Don't you want to go out to dinner?"

"You know you could go out for coffee if you just got vaccinated."

"You're okay to miss out on bowling/the party/the show?"

From that moment, the only opinions that mattered lived under my roof. All decisions I made moving forward were with my family in mind.

This was a decision-defining moment in my life. We have these decisions. Some are small, like saying "I love you," every time you want to because you never know when it will be the last time. Other decisions are bigger, like leaving a secure career you've spent over a decade building. Others are radical, like closing your business, sell-ing your house, and moving your family for more financial security after a scary life event. And some don't even feel like decisions, but a calling you can't deny.

***

"I have three layers of pants on," Sylvia shared as she walked into the house. "Four shirts, a hat, coat and two layers of socks. I'm so hot."

"You're all set," I encouraged her. "Laura May is just in the kitchen. Come on in."

Two of my safest friends were coming together on this freezing cold day. Both of them knew about each other, but they had never met. I knew they would be fast friends. Both single moms of boys, two of the strongest women I knew, both unvaccinated. Sure enough, we could hardly have a conversation between the three of us because we all had too much to say, now that we were finally together.

"We should probably get going," I suggested.

We had been listening to the CB radio for days as the convoy got closer to us. The exact timing of when it would pass was still unclear, but we definitely didn't want to miss it.

We got bundled up and headed out. We had no idea what to expect. My anxiety was high. Where do we stand? Where do we park? What will it be like?

Laura May turned on the tunes and we eased into the drive. Pit-bull's "I Believe That We Will Win" sang through the speakers. I honestly felt like Pitbull telling me that how you get back up is more important than how you fall, was the life affirming mantra that had gotten me through the last four months. This song playing while we drove under the overpass, which was already filled with people, seemed like a scene out of a movie. As we looped around to find parking, we couldn't believe how many cars there were. We found a spot more than a kilometre away. We put on our hats and mitts and started the long walk back to the overpass.

As we approached the crowd, my eyes filled with tears, my heart swelled, and I lost my breath. I hadn't seen a crowd in years, and something I had hidden away popped to the surface, and I started connecting with people by high-fiving as many as possible. As we walked through the crowd, we exchanged smiles with strangers, had moments of laughter, and even gave hugs. Nearly four years after that day on the subway with Marley, I was reminded of the simplicity of connecting with strangers. Human connection really is what it's all about, and I had forgotten that.

We found a spot on the hill beside the 401. There were well over a hundred people there at that point. Children, teens, grandmas and grandpas. People of all kinds, from all over. It was cold but so warm at the same time.

"I missed being around people," Laura May said to us.

"Me too," I responded, and I saw we all had the same tear-filled eyes.

For a few short hours, we stood on the snowy highway hill singing, cheering, and waving our flag. For a few short hours, we had a community of people that understood.

We didn't even need the trucks to drive by; we already knew we were not alone. As the snow fell and the horns honked, I thought to myself, life is good. I didn't know what would come next, but I felt it without fear. I felt it with hope. Hope that I would find my way even if the path was uncertain. Hope that my daughters would be free to create their own paths just as I had. And hope that we will have many new and exciting adventures together, as a family.

Life is good.

COURTNEY HOBBS

Courtney is a mom first and all the other things second. She is a former teacher who loved the students but not the system, so she found herself on a different path than she was taught to want. She is now an entrepreneur who is creating the life she wants. Courtney has been telling stories forever, loves moving her body, and lives for quality time with her family. In her spare time, you can expect to find her connecting with people, baking muffins, or organizing her home.

Courtney would like to thank her husband, Ben, and daughters, Marley and Clarke, for teaching her what this life is all about. She would like to thank her family, who have always done their best to support her, even when it made them feel uncomfortable. She would also like to thank her fellow consciously curious friends, especially Laura May, for being there for it all. And finally, all the people who knew her truth and respected her regardless.

My hope is that
our stories greet you
like a hug full of love
and hope.

♡ *[signature]*

Chapter Thirteen

THE GIRL WHO BROKE FREE

Chelsie Meyers

"Never doubt that a small group of thoughtful,
committed citizens can change the world.
Indeed, it is the only thing that ever has."
–Margaret Mead

On a warm spring day in rural Alberta, a young girl skipped through the yard. There was a dog by her side and two little sisters behind, trying their best to keep up. The lawn was freshly mowed and flowers were planted impeccably in their matching pots. She wore a pretty dress and her hair was pulled back neatly in a bow. You wouldn't find dirt under her fingernails or sand in her perfectly tied shoes. She was to behave, try her best, and follow the rules.

As the young girl grew and she veered off course, feedback hit her right in the heart. To protect herself from the hurt and the shame, the young girl learned how to please. She looked around and would make the choice she assumed others would need.

Once all grown up, the pressure she carried led to anxiety and stress. To cope, she pushed her feelings deep inside and put on a brave face. But ignoring her needs and not following her heart led to much suffering and pain. Then one day a pandemic hit, and suddenly, everything changed . . .

2020

We sat on the couch with looks of disbelief on our faces as the television reported news of a deadly virus spreading rapidly across the globe. The kids would be moving to online school immediately, and my husband would have to work from home. My heart sank, not knowing what to expect and if we would all be okay. We spent the first few weeks glued to the media for updates. I frantically ordered masks and hand sanitizer. I was a bundle of nerves but had faith we could get through this if we listened to the experts and did what we had to do.

After the initial shock wore off, the pressure I had always carried within me slowly started to release. Our calendar was clear and I was able to be home with my family, where I felt the most at ease. I cherished the slower pace and the ability to rest without guilt. Instead of the usual hustle and bustle in the mornings, we awoke to the smell of coffee and the sound of bacon crackling in a pan. Evenings were spent eating together at the table, playing board games, and enjoying one another's company. I looked around at my life; a beautiful home, a hardworking husband, an amazing son and daughter. I was incredibly blessed and it was like I was seeing it all again for the first time. I had gotten so used to going through the motions and doing what was expected of me, that the sudden change had jolted me awake. I began laughing again and found joy in the simple things. We shifted our priorities and reconnected with the true meaning of life. The downtime was restorative and healing.

After the first couple of months, I found myself scrolling social media and began to notice an odd shift. The dire messages of fear and the heart-warming posts that proclaimed "We are all in this together" became diluted by the alternative perspectives that had begun to pop up. Not everyone was lapping up the narrative and differing views started to appear. Negative consequences of lockdowns were being brought to light. I became curious, especially when Big Tech began blocking posts and restricting certain links. I'd see small disclaimer boxes appear below articles or images that didn't align with the mainstream narrative. Influencers started to talk in code so they wouldn't be shadow-banned. Being a rule follower, I continued to 'do my part' but deep down, I knew something was off.

By the time summer rolled around, I was due for a haircut. It had been months since I left the house and my stomach was in knots. When I arrived, my hairstylist opened the door and welcomed me in with a smile. *No mask?* I thought.

"You don't need to wear that thing for me!" she said.

I slipped inside, took the cloth off my face, and went down the stairs to her salon. I'd known my hairstylist for several years and had always admired her authenticity and willingness to tell it like it is. She was never one to shy away from a conversation or pretend to be anything other than herself. I had slowly become the opposite. Unless I felt totally comfortable, I would delicately curate my views to garner acceptance. Somehow, when I sat down in her chair, my true feelings would all come bubbling up. Being around someone so genuine would do that to a person.

Within minutes of my arrival, we began to talk about the pandemic and the government's response. "It's all bullshit," she said. "You think?" I replied, squirming in my seat. She listed off all the things that made absolutely no sense. "Oh my gosh, TOTALLY!" I exclaimed. Holy hell, someone else was questioning all of these things too. A rush of relief fell over me, knowing I was not the only one. Feeling safe to speak freely, conversation poured out of our mouths for the next two hours. We barely took a breath between words as we talked about the covid shenanigans, Hollywood, politics, and the undeniable corruption. We felt like a couple of detectives, drawing feverishly on our giant whiteboard wall. Connecting dots and weaving everything together in our minds. The feeling I had been hiding for weeks was finally validated.

I suspected an agenda was at play and it wasn't the first time I had seen it. After years of my husband working in the Alberta oil and gas industry, we witnessed how lies were used to mislead and shape public opinion. Foreign money and influence had massive impacts on our province. And anyone asking questions or wanting to debate the issues were quickly labelled as 'anti-science' or a 'climate denier.' We could see the same methods of manipulation being used with covid. It was becoming evident that many agendas had been implemented in this way. Governments, corporations, and the media were working together in lockstep. With that realization, trust in our systems and everything as I knew it began to crumble.

As summer came to a close, the public was being bombarded by fear. Daily updates and future modelling were predicting only the most catastrophic outcomes. Not *once* did medical professionals on television try to empower individuals. They did not suggest any healthy interventions such as getting rest, eating well, taking supplements, losing weight, or anything natural that could have helped prevent severe disease. Conversations with our own doctors were alarming. They had serious concerns and were not permitted to speak freely. Common sense went out the window and rules got more ridiculous by the day, but the pressure to comply with the measures was unlike anything I'd ever seen.

In the fall, tensions were high with the lead-up to the US election. After the vote, I was blown away by the irregularities and the media's refusal to even acknowledge them. Very quickly, questioning the election results or covid measures made you open to an attack. A pattern began to emerge. Label anyone disputing the official narrative as racist, misogynistic, or a conspiracy theorist. Demean, shame, and belittle all opposing views. This was the same dismissive tactic I had seen in the past, and it had become an effective way to silence resistance. To me, this felt so wrong. Like most issues facing our society, these topics were very nuanced and complex. Respectful debate was not only within our rights but vital to a healthy democracy. Scrutiny and transparency were imperative in maintaining any sort of trust in our institutions.

I was hesitant to speak out but after seeing the patterns taking shape, I felt it was my only option. I was convinced that once everyone understood that the government was taking advantage of the situation to spread fear and gain control, we could come together to stop it. I passionately voiced my concerns to some friends. To my surprise, I was hit with immediate disapproval. I was ridiculed and gaslit. I was called racist and selfish for not caring about others. It was utterly devastating. Having my character and intelligence questioned by those who had known me for years was like a punch to the gut. Grief began to engulf me. I had spent the last decade carefully managing my emotions. Once the floodgates finally opened, the tears would not stop.

At this same time, I was permanently banned from Twitter for retweets that questioned the government's pandemic response. Imagine that, a platform incapable of preventing child porn but able to block a person for asking simple questions. I was accused of using Twitter in a manner intended to "artificially amplify or suppress information." I wondered, wasn't banning individuals with opposing views doing just that? I appealed it, was denied, and have been banned from ever creating another account. Once again, I had voiced the wrong opinion, it was unacceptable, and I was cancelled. The unprecedented censorship and loss of free speech were unsettling. Being vilified by those close to me was heart-wrenching. That, combined with the apathy of the Canadian public, left me in a state of hopelessness.

2021

The vaccine push began, and even though they told us it did not prevent transmission, the pressure to get it was on. It started with incentives and bribery, and very quickly switched to coercion and intense peer pressure. Having the freedom to make our own medical choices was slipping away, and respect for those choices was becoming a thing of the past.

When you're in a state of fear, it becomes easy to judge a group of 'bad people' you don't know. Especially when political leaders and the media are telling you it's all 'their' fault your life is at risk. But the blame and criticism being thrown at those declining the vaccine were downright cruel. It happened slowly . . . tiny steps at a time . . . and before we knew it, it became socially acceptable to label, condemn, and discriminate. I couldn't believe what was being said on social media. What was happening to kind-hearted and accepting Canadians? Did they realize that many of the 'unvaccinated' were their nieces or nephews? Their coworkers, neighbours, or friends? Could they understand that they had very personal reasons for waiting, or for not wanting the shot? Had they forgotten the goodness within these folks?

Even though I knew people were being manipulated to fear their loved ones, there were certain things said during this time that will be very hard to forget. Some words cut so deep. Despite it all, I strongly believed in the importance of freedom of choice, bodily autonomy, and informed consent. I felt called to do my part in preserving it.

Resisting the pressure to fall in line was difficult and led to more painful consequences. My husband and I were let go from a job we had done together for five years in our spare time. We spent our winter evenings and weekends working hard to support our community and help the local curling rink thrive. My husband was an avid curler and making ice became a passion. When we raised concerns about the vaccine passport that would segregate and turn away twenty percent of our members, we were mocked. When we reluctantly disclosed our personal medical status, we were replaced without even being notified. We were ridiculed for being "freedumb fighters" on social media. The lack of courtesy and disrespect really hurt us. I had decided I would never waver in my decision not to participate in the discriminatory passport program or get the vaccine. But after the humiliation of being cancelled, I learned to shut up about it and not say another word.

Instead, I would watch those who could stomach the vicious attacks speak out online. They would call out the hypocrisy and highlight the government's inconsistencies. I would send them private messages to thank them for their strength and willingness to speak out. One day I received a reply:

I get so many of these messages, and while I appreciate the gratitude, I really wish others would show courage and speak out too.

Ouf. I really felt that. Why should they carry the weight of this alone? And why should I silence myself for the benefit of those in control? Our compliance was their power. I slowly started commenting again and defending the negative attacks. As hard as it was to disappoint family and friends, I was not willing to self-censor when doing so went against every fibre of my being. I had been faced with the ultimate test; cower to meet societal expectations and comply, or draw a line in the sand and stand my ground. It was a people-pleasers worst nightmare. The choice was clear. The pain of going against my values and integrity had become more than the pain of rejection and disapproval.

In the fall, when provincial restrictions were reinstated in schools, I began to strongly voice my concerns in person and on social media. Very quickly, my inbox was filled with messages from other parents who felt the same way. We started emailing school principals and the divisional superintendent. Our school board agreed to let one parent speak at their next meeting, and a friend asked if I would be the one to do it. I was hit with an immediate wave of anxiety but knew it was time for me to step up. I had to speak out for all the parents who had been ignored and for all the distressed teachers facing potential vaccine mandates. Most importantly, I had to advocate for our children. I was not willing to watch them suffer from unnecessary and ineffective measures any longer. The latest restrictions were causing far more harm than good. The growing division and cruel remarks were seeping their way into our schools. I could not look back in regret, knowing I had given into fear and stayed silent.

I sat down to write a letter that outlined my concerns. The words poured out of me in an instant. They had been held in so tightly for months. I shared it with friends from the area, and within days, it spread throughout the division. From town to town, school to school; all by word of mouth. I was blown away by the response and willingness of so many to sign their names in support. I began receiving hundreds of emails and phone calls from moms, dads, grandmas, and grandpas. I heard from teachers, support staff, and community members, each with their own story and reason for supporting my message. Being honest and vulnerable gave others permission to do the same. Families were struggling and their stories were truly devastating. I could feel the pressure so many were under to quit 'rocking the boat' and simply comply. The government's response to this virus was sinister and was causing irreparable harm.

My body shook as I drove to the meeting. Questioning authority had never been easy for me and I was carrying the hopes of many on my shoulders that day. Parents were praying for a common sense approach and a return to normalcy. I knew I had to do my best to convey this to the board. I wanted them to truly see me. To recognize a respectful and level-headed woman. A mother with a benevolent heart who was genuinely concerned about her children and their teachers. I wasn't there to cause trouble or make waves, my intention was to represent all the salt-of-the-earth families who had been cast away. The media had depicted us as a bunch of self-centred lunatics, but that was not who we were. I wanted the board to look past the policies on paper, to see a real face, and to remember their humanity.

I paused and took one last deep breath before entering the building. I was led down a long hallway, weaving in and around offices, eventually making our way to the board room. I was to stand in the doorway to deliver my remarks. Every trustee was sitting socially distanced around a giant circle of tables. Each one had their mask on, with tiny plates of half-eaten pieces of cake by their sides.

I asked if I could take off my mask and, after a unanimous vote, was able to remove it. The place was so quiet you could hear a pin drop. These were the people in charge of making the decisions that directly affected our children, and you could tell it had been a long time since a parent had attended one of their meetings. I was given three minutes to present my concerns and then was whisked away as quickly as I had arrived.

I know our message had an impact on the board, but the top-down approach to policy-making in our education system left them with little power to do much about it. To continue to fight for local autonomy, it became a full-time job speaking with administrators, trustees, health and safety departments, advocacy groups, and MLAs. Everyone I spoke to said they understood our concerns, but their "hands were tied." I heard this same line over and over again. Every conversation only led to more unanswered questions, but they *all* knew me by name and understood I was *not* going away.

To foster accountability, networking with parents became crucial. Due to mounting censorship on social media, we created groups by email or on alternative platforms like Telegram. We compiled the latest data and studies being ignored by the media to pass on to leadership. We started petitions and mass email campaigns. We vented our frustrations and encouraged each other to carry on. An underground movement of concerned and engaged citizens was growing across the country, but because it was never spoken about on the news, most Canadians had no clue.

In early December, I was invited to a meeting held in a rural hall on the Alberta prairies. The meeting included groups and individuals from around the province. Doctors, lawyers, pastors, farmers, business owners, teachers, nurses, political candidates, police officers, paramedics, and more. Hardly a fringe minority. I was honoured to be included.

These were some of the most inspiring and genuine humans I have ever met. They were the canaries in the coal mine. The ones who saw through the deception and understood the importance of standing up and speaking out now. We had come together to share our unique perspectives and abilities to carve out a path forward. We were treated to an amazing meal cooked by a few lovely ladies from a nearby community. It felt incredible to be doing something 'normal' again. Helping ourselves to a smorgasbord of delicious home-cooked food, desserts, coffee, and tea felt like a simple pleasure from the past.

To be in a room with those open to conversation was an amazing feeling after all the months of isolation and despair. Many I had connected with virtually and it felt incredible to finally hug and meet in person. These remarkable people knew what we were up against and they were in it for the long haul. For me, there was no turning back. I refused to cower in fear again and knew which side of history I would be on.

2022

Excitement and hope were restored when thousands of quiet, obedient citizens finally took that brave step out of the shadows to make themselves known. Canadians came out in droves to support the truckers in their movement for freedom of choice. Families cheered on the sides of highways and on overpasses, dressed in red and waving their Canadian flags. Seeing the love, kindness, and relief on their faces was astounding and brought tears to my eyes.

Of course, the government and media twisted it like they always do, but they cannot take away or make us forget the reality of what we saw. We witnessed the genuine spirit and patriotic hearts of Canadians. We are capable of greatness and have been controlled by division and fear. We were lulled into complacency and conditioned to be the compliant people they needed us to be. The only thing any of us ever needed to be was our innate selves.

When we stand by our values and beliefs, we are challenging the corrupt systems that have been put in place and held over us for generations. This is what many of us have been called to do. So to all those who lead with grace, love, and authenticity: *thank you*. Your example has inspired me to do the same. I have faith that together we will build systems of integrity and change this world beyond our wildest dreams.

The truth is, 'cancel culture' and government overreach gave me the resolve to break free from my own mind. To stop living for everyone else and start living in alignment with my true self. Going against the grain released the deep fear the young girl within me had of rejection and disapproval. I'm learning to honour my intuition and to move through life with intention, gently stepping out of old patterns and into new ways of being.

Despite the punitive restrictions still in place, the woman I am today is the freest I've ever been. I finally understand that there is more to life than simply existing and following the path of predictability. I'm unearthing all that fuels my soul and lights me up inside. At age forty, I have released the chains of perfection and the need to please. I am following my heart, owning my sovereignty, discovering my life's purpose, and embracing all that is to come.

CHELSIE MEYERS

Chelsie Meyers is a recovering perfectionist who is releasing herself from societal expectations and stepping into her authenticity. With a strong sense of curiosity and justice, she has spent hours researching everything from natural healing and holistic health to geopolitics and government corruption. Chelsie went from burning out in the educational system as a teacher, to tackling it head-on as a parent a decade later. Parents are key stakeholders in public education, and she is on a mission to restore that role. Chelsie's ultimate goal is to live in alignment with her best self, trusting her intuition, opening her heart, and flowing in a state of simplicity and ease. As a lifelong learner, she continues to pursue her passions, expand her mind, and discover her life's purpose. She lives in a small Alberta town with her supportive husband Kerry, their two amazing children, Ben and Lia, and their dog, Stella.

Thank you to my husband for knowing and accepting all of me. You are my safe place.

To my children, the two bright lights in my life. Your genuine hearts shine through in all you do. I love you both, just as you are.

Thank you to my parents for all your love and support. You have always stood by your values and beliefs. Your strength and courage inspire me.

To my sisters and their families for always allowing me to be me, thank you.

I am blessed to have friends who knew me long before I lost myself. Thank you for guiding me home.

To my hairstylist and dear friend who sparked an awakening within me on that fateful summer day, thank you. You are a precious gift to this world.

Finally, to all the amazing people I have connected with since 2020. We are bonded for life. No one truly understands the journey we've been on. I admire each and every one of you for being brave, speaking your truth, and inspiring others to do the same.

Be fearlessly authentic♡
Chelsu Meyer

Chapter Fourteen

MARIPOSA

Ashley Correia

—She found her voice in solitude and nature. A place to rest her magnetic heart and allow the complexity of her soul to feel at ease. She surrendered to places her mind never led her, but only her soul could. She stopped telling herself stories and started writing them. Her saving grace became the death of herself—

I looked across the table at my cousins at my dad's retirement party. They were smiling, whispering and watching me interact with my niece and nephew. I heard them talking about the 'new me,' who everyone calls 'Cottage Ash.' The calm, free-thinking, leading with love version of me. Sometimes I don't even recognize myself. I have this ease and playfulness in me now, a feeling of safety in my body and in my thoughts. I still double-take when I make decisions from this place because it is unfamiliar to me and to the people around me. Up until now, I had been giving far too much voice to my grief, programmed beliefs about myself, and irrational fears, while seeking the guidance of external sources. To outsiders, I had everything I could have ever wanted in my life and all that my parents strived for me to have: stability. Or at least, their markers of it. I had a good education, a well-paying career, a beautiful family, and a nice home. Yet, I was the most powerless I had ever been. Floating out and on top of myself, not living in my body, being consumed by ruminating thoughts and worries and grasping for a sense of peace. Some women call these the dark days of the night, and they were aplenty for me. But yet here I sit, the most sovereign and free version of myself, during the most restricted time in my country, ready to spread my wings and fly wherever love will take me.

***

Therapy has been a life-changing experience for me. Although I have gone to therapy a few different times in my life, with a few different therapists, for a few different reasons, none compare to my experience over the last three years. I started seeing a new therapist when my son Caden was just two months old. This, sadly, was the darkest moment of my life. Simply just *being* felt impossible. I was dealing with crippling postpartum anxiety and depression. It had peaked when Caden was born, but truthfully, it had been on a slow rise since becoming a mother to my first son, Colby, a few years prior. On the day I went into labour with Caden, I woke up with a "cold sore." For all I know, it could have been a blister from labour approaching and all of the many hormones coursing through my body. But it didn't matter, because my mind told me that this cold sore virus would kill Caden. And I believed it.

The mind is a very powerful storyteller. I started covering the cold sore up with a patch and tape. So much tape that I couldn't even open my mouth to eat, and smoothies were the only things I consumed. I worried that if I left my cold sore uncovered, the germs would spread to the air and onto my son. The worry took up all of the real estate in my thoughts, making it difficult to heal from birth and to nourish my newborn child. I became obsessed and completely unaware of my extreme behaviours. My mind told me that everything I was doing was necessary to keep Caden healthy and alive, and these ruminating thoughts did not take a day off. Soon my behaviours slowly became more obsessive and compulsive. I used plastic dishes and utensils so I could dispose of my germs. I cleaned the shower after every use, put towels over my pillow case and changed them every time I rested my head. I over-cleaned and over-sanitized. I planned out every event in my future and how I could remain in control of the germs. It didn't end there, though. I saw other people as a threat to Caden, too. My mind assumed that everyone around me was carrying a virus that could hurt him. Including my firstborn son. I still carry sadness about how I treated Colby during this time, who was only three and a half years old. He would so much as sneeze in the room and I would take Caden and me under the covers, visibly panicked, but avoiding the germs. I give myself compassion now looking back, but I still worry about the impact of my irrational fears on Colby's growing perception of safety in himself and the world. Even now, I walk around this current world and think about the impact of the last few years on this generation of children and their inner safety.

Eventually, my mind told me that I was going to die too, instigated by the fear of leaving my children without me there to keep them safe. I became hyper-focused on every last symptom or sensation in my body and convinced myself daily that I was harbouring disease and, worst case scenario, cancer. At one point, every washroom in my house had a flashlight on the counter so I could obsessively stare at my throat, examine its spots and lumps, convincing myself that I had throat cancer. It's like my brain would go to the worst-case scenario in order to protect myself from the pain of it coming true because "I've already lived it in my mind." I think all moms do this at times. At this point, though, my midwives became worried. My family became worried. I became worried. On top of the time constraints of breastfeeding, I literally . . . couldn't . . . sleep! I think it was the insomnia that really almost killed me. Looking back now, I can completely understand. My nervous system was an absolute mess, living in a constant state of fight or flight. No wonder I couldn't sleep. In my body and my mind, it felt like I was being chased by a lion. To escape it, I lived outside of my body, trying not to physically feel it. As a result, I spent all of my time in my brain, in the darkness created by spiralling thoughts. At the one-month mark, it was clear that this was not just a case of the baby blues. I needed help. And after a particular bout of insomnia that lasted for seventy-two hours straight, I took action and reached out for support to anyone who could help. This was the first step I took in developing my own abundant self-trust, which at this time was completely non-existent.

My first call was to my family doctor. She had been my doctor my whole life, and we had an interesting relationship. She always treated me like I was over worrying about things. With this condescending tone, she'd say, "Oh, Ashley!" Often telling me that my worry and pain were all in my head. On that winter day, though, at rock bottom, I sobbed hysterically to her, "I need help." I often wonder if having him in the cold, dark winter made this all worse. She recommended medication, to start immediately. Zoloft for depression and anxiety, and lorazepam for three weeks to calm my nervous system and brain so that I could sleep. It worked. I was breastfeeding, though, and already incredibly fearful about anything hurting Caden. I worried about what the medication could do to him through my breast milk. Breastfeeding was one of the few things that gave me purpose. In all of the hardships breastfeeding gave me, it also gave me comfort, and I would not give it up. At least the medications that were prescribed were "breastfeeding safe." Although let's be honest, the acid reflux medication that I was recommended to take during both of my pregnancies, said to be safe, ended up being linked with cancer and taken off the market. So, as I have done for most of my life, when a decision carries a lot of weight, I sought out more information. I was referred to the postpartum anxiety clinic at the hospital for a second opinion. Here I met with a psychiatrist who diagnosed me with Generalized Anxiety Disorder and Obsessive-Compulsive Disorder. No surprise there; remember the plastic cutlery and flashlights? She prescribed me similar medications as my family doctor, albeit at much higher doses, which was so confusing in an already confusing state. But I went on the meds so that I could do the real work in therapy, and I am still so grateful for that decision. I can barely even write this because it hurts my heart so much, but while going through all of this, I wouldn't let myself kiss either of my children because I thought my germs could hurt them. I didn't kiss Caden for the first time until he was four months old. Nowadays, I kiss them both a million times a day, just because.

My first appointment with my therapist was in March 2019, when

Caden was almost two months old. I still have the notes from all of our sessions in my journals. I plan on sharing the important teachings and learnings one day, I'm just not sure how yet. The therapist's office was in a medical building. The kind with a pharmacy, walk-in clinic, bloodwork clinic, with people who are sick. My worst nightmare. Virtual appointments didn't exist back then. To get to his office, I had to walk through the upstairs, into the basement and down the hall. This meant multiple handles to touch and many people to walk by and hold my breath past. In our second session together, my therapist introduced me to Anny, the guard of my nervous system. This intro-duction was the single most profound chapter in my journey back to myself. At first, my therapist made me carry around a small toy in my pocket to acknowledge Anny as something that will always be there, but separate from me. Because she needs to be. Anny uses the information signals from my mind and body and decides whether to activate fight or flight mode. Anny is responsible for ramping up my sympathetic nervous system, igniting a whole-body response, so that I can run from the lion when in danger. She is crucial to my survival. Unfortunately, she was much too overbearing once Caden was born, and she signalled everything as a threat, even as small as a cough. We spent months understanding Anny in therapy. What was she up to, and how could I learn to tolerate her? I began separating myself from Anny's thoughts. Her thoughts were not mine. I told my family and friends about her. I asked them to point out when they thought Anny was having too much of a say, which they did with love. First, this looked like me saying to my husband, "Is me avoiding that play place this weekend Anny talking?" Of which, with zero judgment, he would confirm. I ran with this idea. Analyzing whose voice, mine or Anny's, was making the decisions. More importantly, if the decisions being made aligned with my family values, which was another technique taught in therapy. Slowly, I became an observer of my thoughts, emotions, and behaviours. Seeing them for what they were without judgment. My therapist calls this "Name it to tame it" or "Thanks, Anny, for that information. I've got this, though." For me, retraining my thought patterns was not enough, though. I also had to deal with my Obsessive-Compulsive behaviours (OCD), which were getting worse and making it hard to live day to day. Whenever I make any bit of progress, Anny feels like she is losing control, so she pushes back. Luckily for me now, I see what she's up to!

My therapist and I started exposure work almost immediately to deal with the OCD thoughts and behaviours. At first, my homework would be as simple as delaying until I got to the car to sanitize my hands after our therapy session ended. Then he would add that I had to touch all the door handles on the way out. Sometimes I had to delay changing my clothes when I got home from his office. Then he would add hugging my husband with my 'Out in Public' clothes. Next, we did half of what my mind requested. For example, I could only look at my throat two out of the four times that I went into the bathroom. Eventually, I had to take some flashlights out of the bathrooms. Each step in pushing my comfort zone was a very slow process. I had so many OCD behaviours, outside of the ones mentioned above. Doing half, or even delaying, any of what my mind was telling me was incredibly uncomfortable physically, mentally, and emotionally. Therapy is not a walk in the park. Eventually, when my body could handle it, we got to the deeper exposure work. Anny had created a small comfort zone for me to stay safe in, and I had to stretch it. If I didn't, then I would not be able to make memories with my beautiful family, and that was my driving value, the compass for my decisions. During these exposure sessions, my therapist and I walked around the medical building. He would have me sit in one of the bloodwork chairs in the lab. Or touch the handles in the public bathroom. Each time, the same thing would happen. A tight chest, racing heart, sweaty palms, and hot face. My therapist coached me to feel the painful physical sensations in my body, acknowledge them, and then breathe deeply, signalling safety to Anny. One exposure at a time, one breath at a time, I got less and less of a bodily reaction. My comfort zone got bigger and bigger. I was learning to regulate my nervous system. This made Anny angry. Every time progress was made, Anny would get louder in my thoughts, catastrophize bigger, or choose something new to focus on. For example, if she noticed me becoming unafraid of germs, she would 'cherry pick' and replay past events over and over and over in my mind, making me relive everything. Each time I would tell her, "I hear you, Anny, but I've got this. I'm safe." Doing the work in therapy and being accountable to the homework changed my thought patterns in ways I never knew possible, and I began my journey to feeling safe in my body. I am in the driver seat now, and Anny is thankfully riding in the back, some days in the trunk. Everyone has an Anny, a voice that has too much of a say in personal decisions, maybe a perfectionist voice or a voice of self-doubt. Getting curious about any voices speaking too loud freed me, and ultimately my heart leads the conversations now.

Even though I knew what Anny was up to, in order to fully challenge my thinking, I needed to understand why Anny behaved the way she did and what she was so afraid of. I feel like this was trauma work. The more I learned about Anny, the more I could understand and tolerate her, which was necessary for keeping her in the back seat. On the most obvious level, Anny emerged to stay one step ahead and keep my precious babies safe. But deeper than that, my own struggle with fertility and pregnancy loss exacerbated the miracle to which Anny was born to protect.

My first pregnancy ended in miscarriage. The loss of connection I had formed with this growing fetus and the emotional grief from my visions of the future being wiped clean, coupled with the physical sensations of purging tissue that once was a life, opened the door wide open for Anny to arrive. Although this loss was one of the deepest, I am still grateful for it. If it didn't happen, I wouldn't have my son Colby, my most sweet and gentle soul. A few years after having Colby, we wanted another baby. I struggled to get pregnant. This had never been an issue with the first two pregnancies. Months after months of cycle tracking, and after seeking professional help, the verdict was in. My egg count was low, my autoimmune thyroid disease had been messing up my hormones, and my surgery on my ovary in my twenties had built up scar tissue that affected the follicles. *"We will try to get you another, but be grateful you have one,"* the words of the fertility doctor still haunt us. I started with different fertility medications to increase my follicles or production of eggs, but they had so many awful side effects. One of the medications gave me terrifying night blindness. We also tried IUI, but it was unsuccessful. I was struggling to balance all of the appointments and procedures, while teaching Kindergarten full time and raising Colby. I was tired. So, I opted for IVF to have the best chances. I was lucky enough to afford it. From an entire round of IVF, the bloodwork, intravaginal ultrasounds, needles, hormones, and operating rooms, I got ONE viable embryo. Just one. Plus, it still had to stick, and with my history of miscarriage, this was not a guarantee. That one viable embryo is Caden, my fearless boy, his name meaning *warrior,* and he figuratively and literally ripped me open upon his arrival. It is no wonder Anny swooped in.

A year after starting therapy and making some incredible gains with my germ and illness anxiety, covid arrived. It was March 2020. My very fear was coming true; germs actually *could* kill my children. We were not safe. It was like my postpartum experience was a simulation exercise in order for me to develop the skills needed to make it through. At first, we knew nothing about covid, only what the media and world were telling us . . . *A Global Pandemic.* Stay in your homes. Stop your life. Don't see your family. For the first three months of the pandemic, we followed all the rules. We sanitized bananas, wore masks, and stayed at home. Caden was only one and Colby was four. I am still haunted by how quickly we taught our children not to run up to our parents and hug them when we were out in the backyard for our socially distanced visits. Anny's voice was loud again. Only this time, it wasn't just me. In fact, all of society seems to have Obsessive-Compulsive Disorder: Crossing the road when walking by others outside, over-sanitizing every public surface, following arrows on the floors, wearing masks, wiping down their groceries, to name a few. It wasn't just Anny being hypervigilant now, everyone was, so it was even harder to kick her to the back seat when the world was giving her the stage. The safety that I had developed in myself through extremely hard and honest work in therapy was not enough to navigate this new world. The sheer panic of people around me, and the familiarity of fear controlling the narrative, led me deep into the weeds. That dark place again, with a limited amount of hope. So, as I usually do when discomfort in life feels heavy, I got curious and asked questions. I became thirsty for information on all sides of covid to silence Anny. I then assessed my own low personal risk of serious illness from covid. 'Facts over fear' became my motto, which I teach to my children now. Although Anny got louder at times because the world was giving her a microphone, I seemed to be looking at the world differently than everyone else. Luckily, fear was not going to run my life again. My values were too important.

I remember the day we decided to surprise our parents with hugs from our children. It had been nine long weeks since they had hugged. I remember when the boys went with open arms toward my mother-in-law. I can still hear her uncontrollable sobs in my head. I am surprised she was able to stay standing. The same thing happened with my dad. Caden was heading towards a prickly bush, and my dad was screaming "Ash, Ash, Ash" because he was closest but wasn't *allowed* to touch him. I said, "Dad, just pick him up." My dad balled his eyes out while lifting and hugging him. I can still see them standing in front of that prickly bush, although my eyes were full of tears. These are the stories that we all have. All of us, on every side of every issue. We *all* gave up a lot!

* * *

In the fall of 2021, I felt very alone. While I had overcome my fear of the virus itself, I was now facing a new fear: rejection from society. At this time, there were two categories which determined your access to society: the vaccinated and the unvaccinated. You can guess which group I belong to. Informed consent with my body is not something I take lightly, as you know. Unfortunately, the Prime Minister didn't care. He wanted me to take a personal risk that I didn't need. All for the Greater Good, whatever that is. My research into other countries that rolled out the vaccine before us showed early on that the vaccine did not reduce transmission, even though our experts said otherwise. And yet, my choice not to get it cost me almost everything. Around this time, *The Toronto Star* put an article on their front cover saying: "We have no empathy left for the unvaccinated. Let them die." Colleagues in my school board Facebook group shared the article proudly. The same group of people who fight equity like it is their *only* job as educators, but not this time. Policies in my teaching job were discriminatory, requiring me to test three times a week, while vaccinated colleagues who were catching and spreading covid, did not have to. I couldn't even take my children to their favourite activities. I lost friendships and relationships quickly and vastly, being labelled as selfish, reckless, misinformed, tinfoil hat wearer, and conspiracy theorist. Friends attacked me on social media saying, "You should just suck it up and get the vaccine." Others whispered to my loved ones, "Is Ashley going crazy?" Some days I really thought I might be. I remember when my doctor told me that "clearly my OCD was acting up again, since I knew too much about covid and the vaccine." The gaslighting continued. I was seeing more darkness than light again. Participating in the covid charade was hurting my soul, so I took a leave of absence from my job as a Kindergarten teacher. Not a decision I took lightly, but one that was necessary for my mental health. I cocooned with my family for months while the media, government, and society labelled me a misogynist, sexist, racist, misinformed, and of course, selfish. I wish they could see me in my Kindergarten classroom, in my element, pouring love all day long to my students, families, and colleagues. It really was a tough realization that people weren't perceiving me the way I really was and were putting me into boxes that didn't make sense or even exist. All I ever wanted was for my informed decision to be respected, like I respected the decisions others made for themselves. Eventually, I realized that the only way to navigate this judgy world was by letting go of my concern over what others thought about me. Nobody was going to perceive me as I was, my truth was mine, and their truth was theirs. In the process of releasing layers of my identity that were there to serve others, I found my own authentic self. It was hidden under my identity as a perfectionist and type A overachiever; qualities based on my ego that were no longer serving my highest potential. The harder the government and outside world tried to restrict me, the deeper I got in my values and the closer I was to my own personal sovereignty. I was finally free to be me.

What came next was a physical change to my appearance, something visual to represent my transformation. In December 2021, I finally got my first tattoo. I had been dreaming it up for a while. But I had been too afraid of being judged, especially by the parents of the students that I teach. I was worried that they would judge my ability to take care of their child because of their stereotypes of people with tattoos. Their trust in me is something I value. Instead, the opposite has happened. My tattoo has actually become such a great conversation starter, an ice breaker, for me to share the story, in the guise of explaining my tattoo.

This builds trust. The DNA strand in my tattoo leads up and turns into the tree roots of the large Bonsai in the distance, representing my family. My roots. Nature. The tree also has symbolism to the one we stood under when we got the call from the fertility clinic that Caden had stuck, that we were pregnant. Symbolising the beginning of our family tree. I save that detail about the story for those closest to me.

The butterflies around the tree represent transformation. My transformation. Butterflies have always been my symbol of spirit. There are also four of them to represent my family.

The lily in the tattoo represents my rebirth and death cycle, very fitting for my journey.

Then there is the chandelier, the show stopper in my opinion, a mix of candles and jewels, representing light. My true magic. Me as the lighthouse.

This tattoo, my first tattoo, a very visible half sleeve, took two days and fourteen hours to complete. Every bit of pain, sometimes intense, released old parts of me that no longer served me, until I was left with a badass tattoo and my most authentic self.

Becoming curious about my thoughts, feelings, and emotions without judgment, liberated me in many ways. Finding my authentic self gave me my voice. But coming back into my body, listening to it communicate, and regulating my nervous system after years of motherhood, really solidified my personal freedom. I started with yoga, meditation, reiki, and my most familiar modality, acupuncture, tuning into the frequency and energy of my body, and learning to use breath as medicine. I tapped into the magnetic energy of women around me on similar journeys of self-study and made real connections and honest relationships a priority. Recently, on a beautiful sunny day, I spent the day with a group of women, including my sister, bestie, and cousin, on the floor of a milk farm, doing yoga, meditation, reiki, and journaling together. So much power came from women sharing our own personal journeys with one another. I continue my journey of coming home to myself through my sessions with Abigail, my spiritual advisor. She helps me speak with my body, or my 'soma' as she calls it. She creates a safe space for my emotions, feelings, and physical sensations to come up. Through breathing, dancing, bouncing, punching, screaming, singing, and chanting, we move the energy out, leaving me feeling peaceful, safe, and able to lead with love, my ultimate form of communication. Only in the last few months have I integrated safety into my body. True safety. Not only to show up as I authentically am, but also safe to live in the present. Safe to live in the gray, the neutral, the day-to-day. Not dwelling on any parts of any previous decisions. And in my case, not letting my thoughts spend too much time thinking about things that are uncertain or out of my control. I honoured my gut feelings, whether it was a yes or a no. I can see first-hand that I am co-creating the most magnificent life with a power that is beyond what meets the eye. Three years later, today, I sit in our family trailer, having sold our forever home before finding the next one, and having resigned from our careers in pursuit of a life outside of the rat race. I am now the woman with no plan, peacefully watching life unfold, making amazing memories with my three boys and acting on opportunities that align with our family values. I have abundant self-trust. A far cry from the girl who hoarded flashlights. As Dorothy learned, I had it in me all along! I cannot wait for what is in store for my family and I, in this very strange and divided, yet unbelievably beautiful, world.

—*She thought about the last two years and heard "It's later than you think." She remembered the true lesson as of late: the gift of time and the opportunity to experience it with a full heart. That became her ultimate pursuit, making memories in the moment, at every stage of life! The world will bend when you're ready. She smiled and walked off hand and hand with her three boys!*—

ASHLEY CORREIA

Ashley is a Canadian mom and wife navigating this ever-changing world and figuring out the best way to raise her two beautiful boys. Although fear almost took her life, with a lot of help and even more personal work, she embarked on a journey to sovereignty. She left her overachieving, people-pleasing, perfectionist self behind. Now she is a woman with an abundance of belief, who is letting life unfold for her and her family upon the values of love, curiosity, and communication! Ashley has been teaching primary aged children for twelve years in a large public board in Ontario. Most of her career was spent teaching Kindergarten, ages four to six. This is where her heart lies and her light shines. She also has a degree in Psychology (University of Western Ontario) and a Master's degree in Teaching (OISE, University of Toronto). Recently, Ashley and her family moved from the GTA to Huntsville, Ontario in order to enjoy a slower pace of life, be closer to nature, build a homestead, and find her community. You will find her bike riding, writing, doing yoga, floating in the ocean or lake, going on daily adventures with her family, and travelling around Canada in her family trailer. Follow Ashley on Instagram @IamAshleyCorreia for her honest reflection on raising a family in this current Canada and to see where the next chapter leads her sovereign family in this weird and wonderful world.

Thanks to my hubby for holding down the fort while I poured my soul and story onto paper. Without your support, I would not have found my love for writing. I would also like to thank my village of family and friends for supporting me, as they always do. Thank you to the healers, professionals, and mentors who helped catapult my growth in my journey of self-discovery. And to my boys for inspiring me daily to show up as the highest and most authentic version of myself. Lastly, I want to thank Sarah for allowing me to be a part of such an incredible movement and message of finding our personal freedom, true expression and voice, in a time when it is difficult to do so. I know we will all move many hearts with our stories!

You can't have a Rainbow,
Without a little Rain!

Ashley Correia

Chapter Fifteen

THE GREAT PARADOX

Sarah Swain

The snow crunched beneath our feet as we turned and embraced each other in the cold darkness of the night. I had never hugged him so tightly and I could feel a lump moving from my stomach up into my throat. My eyes stung as I struggled to hold back the tears and I knew he was experiencing the same. We kissed each other and as our eyes met, we both saw the pain and anger we were holding back. He reluctantly walked me to the truck he had ready and warm for me and as I climbed into the driver's seat, I swallowed the lump and pushed it down as far as I could. I didn't want him to worry about me, even though I knew he had every right to. *What on earth was I thinking?* I buckled up and gave him one last kiss before I closed the door, put the truck in drive and slowly drove away. As soon as our home was no longer in the rearview mirror, I allowed the tears to flow. It was 3:45 am on January 24, 2022, and I was heading to Ottawa.

***

Who made these rules, anyway?

The world had stopped making sense to me around 2014, as I waged a war within myself over the meaning of success. I was a ladder-climbing force in the corporate world and was learning that the higher I climbed, the more miserable I became. I grappled with understanding why so much weight was put on career, benefits, pension, home ownership, and relationship status – instead of things like health, happiness, fulfilment, and time. I had everything that made me successful by society's definition, yet I didn't feel anything remotely close to it. Trading our precious time in exchange for money felt like a prison to me. I was thirty years old and wondering if this was all life was, confused about why we had accepted it as a society. Why did we allow so much of ourselves and our life experience to be controlled by a bi-weekly paycheque? Why forty hours a week? Why eight to twelve hours a day? Why Monday to Friday? Why nine to five? Who invented weekends? WTF is time anyway?! *I felt crazy challenging such societal norms.* I would watch everyone I knew go about their work days without questioning a single thing and I found out as I shared my own thoughts, questioning the workforce was somehow synonymous with being ungrateful for one's paycheque. Wanting more out of life, synonymous with a lack of appreciation of one's current life. We can be grateful for what we have, and still want more, can't we? My views seemed to make people uncomfortable, as they contradicted their own life path. Was I just another annoying millennial questioning the way the world worked? Was I the problem? The more I questioned the status quo, the more I realized it wouldn't work for me. Yet at the time, I couldn't see any other option.

So off I'd go, day after day, ensuring that the over-the-counter drugs were selling like hotcakes, and auditing pharmacies to protect them from government clawbacks. I worked in an industry that measured its success on script counts and injections and relied on people to continue to need them. The misalignment was very, very real for me.

As I pushed through year after year in my career, the sense of suffocation from feeling trapped in a career that felt opposite to my values system grew more and more intense. I'd wake up in the morning, put my feet on the floor, adorn a figurative mask, go to work, come home, remove the mask, and spend the remainder of my evening stressed about the day ahead that hadn't even happened yet. Wine and chips were my choice of therapy. Groundhog Day wasn't just a movie. It was my life. I felt like I had been tricked. I had done everything right. I went to school. Got good grades. Got a great job. Got married. Bought a home. Had paid vacation. Benefits. Pension. *Job security, right?* I had ridden this bloody assembly line of life like a good girl, and it felt like I couldn't get off. I thought I was free, but I was only free within the walls of the cage I had built around myself. The walls of my cage were made of societal expectations, the desire to fit in, to be approved of, and ultimately, to belong. I didn't understand it at the time, but these basic human wants and behaviours had imprisoned me in a life that didn't even remotely fit who I was on the inside. After a brief leave of absence in 2017, I threw my middle finger to the man and made the decision to take control of my own life path. I quit my six-figure job and never looked back. I chose freedom and self-trust in the face of uncertainty, over spending another moment living on someone else's terms.

I was free.

***

You can't say that on the internet.

Little did I know, that just two years into my business journey, a familiar feeling would return. The feeling that someone else was at the wheel. Like I couldn't actually do all the things I wanted to do. Or say all the things I wanted to say. It was almost as if I had a boss again, hanging over my shoulder, breathing down my neck, making sure I operated on their terms. *Cancel culture had arrived.* An intense narrative was forming, followed by mob-like behaviours from people who could not accept diversity of thought, or regulate themselves when confronted with an opposing view. Something had shifted in our world and I suddenly felt like I was trapped in a box again. I had never felt like I needed to hide my political views before, but suddenly I did. The media was on a war path to destroy Trump's presidency and Andrew Scheer was going toe-to-toe with Trudeau in the 2019 election. I could see so clearly how the media was effective in shaping the thoughts of the general public when it came to right-wing politicians as slowly the public began to follow suit and condemn anyone who appeared to support them. The media said, "Jump!" And the public started to respond with, "how high?!" It infuriated me, as I was more informed on politics than most and the media's attempt at discrediting any threat to leftist political powers was palpable . . . and unfortunately, effective.

By May 2020, we had been stuck in our homes for weeks, glued to our television screens and mobile devices to gobble up any updates on the pandemic. So, when the largest social justice movement of our generation began to roll across the globe, something insidious seemed to ride in its wake. While the world bellowed for justice, equality, and acceptance, there was another storm brewing. As I did my best to learn and understand the pain the Black community was experiencing, I couldn't help but notice another form of intolerance beginning to form. Intolerance of thought and speech. Any form of nuanced dialogue about the social justice movement was met with a swift *cancellation* of a person or their business. We had normalised the destruction of another human being for asking questions, holding a different view, or failing to use their platforms in ways society demanded. How was this uniting us? Was this not creating more division? Was this really about accountability, or were we all pawns in another game of political chess? I could feel my throat closing as any shred of safety in self-expression was gone from our world, unless it fell in line with legacy media's position on any issue - the most powerful entity on earth. The enormous role the government and media were playing in the mass scale social division we were witnessing sent chills up my spine. Not only was a wedge being driven into our world under the guise of unity and justice, but true acts of racism were getting lost amidst the battle of the most virtuous. We had lost the point and been led astray. By the end of 2020, it felt nothing like social justice and everything like social control. Why was no one else seeing this? Or were they, and just too afraid to say something . . . like me?

I felt anything but free.

***

They developed a vaccine.

While society seemed to be breathing a collective sigh of relief at the news of a vaccine for Covid-19, the hair on the back of my neck was standing on end. My concern and skepticism for the pandemic itself, and the government's clear desire to divide us, was growing. As everyone was excited to return to normal, I was eager to find more information. I felt alarmed by the rate at which the vaccine was developed and labelled with safety and efficacy. I was even more concerned by the fact that it sure didn't seem like we were allowed to ask any questions. This felt familiar . . . It may have been my intuition. It may have been my skepticism of the pharmaceutical industry's goals and intentions from my career experience. It may have been the unbelievably obvious government divide and conquer power grab because of how closely I paid attention to politics. It may have been the unnecessary level of fear being instilled in the population for a virus with an extremely high survival rate. It may have been my observation of the political weaponization of social justice movements. It may have been all of the above. But something told me to start digging. And that's how I landed on VAERS. The Vaccine Adverse Event Reporting System is run by the CDC, Center for Disease Control. While it only provided data for Americans, at least it was something. In fact, it was the only form of raw data I could find. Everything else was friendly pamphlets and government websites touting that we could get back to normal soon – yay vaccine!

I digress.

I quickly learned how to perform a search in the VAERS public database and hit the button to submit my query, which was simply a selection of the Covid-19 vaccine, sorted by symptoms. After a few moments, an enormous list of symptoms appeared on my screen, in alphabetical order. I was shocked at the size of the list, especially given that the vaccine had barely been out for about two months at the time of my search. When I scrolled to "D", I remember my heart skipping a beat. Death. Next to the word *death* appeared a number that made me shake my head and question whether I was seeing my screen right. It couldn't be right. Or maybe it was? And maybe that was just normal? What did I know about vaccines anyway? So I decided to run a search on the more popular vaccines that most people in America likely received. Measles, Mumps, Rubella, Polio . . . In a strange way, I was hoping that the numbers I was seeing on the Covid-19 vaccines would be justified in the adverse reaction results for these other vaccines. Not the case . . . Not even close. *How on earth are these covid vaccines being released to the public? Aren't they supposed to share the risks associated like they do with every other drug? People need to be informed about this, don't they? How many deaths are too many deaths for a new vaccine?* I was spinning. Something wasn't right. And it wasn't long before doctors started speaking up all over the world, sharing the same information I was seeing on the screen that day. *Phew.* I felt so relieved to know I wasn't the only one with major concerns as more and more images of band-aids on arms started flooding my feeds. Yet one by one, the doctors speaking up were wiped clean off the internet, long before people ever got a chance to hear what they had to say. Gone. Disappeared. Branded as danger-ous medical professionals gone rogue. Licenses stripped. *Cancelled.* The only people who seemed to be making any sense to me were being silenced. What was even worse, is that the public appeared to accept the vilification of medical professionals for sharing a different perspective from the media and the government. Freedom of speech had officially become something to fear, instead of protect. We had been primed for these times.

I have to say something.

The fact that I needed to perform a risk analysis when choosing to speak up told me everything I needed to know about how far I had fallen from my perception of my own personal freedom. While I had freed myself from the workforce and had full control over how I spent my time and the life I was creating, I wasn't free at all if I couldn't use my own voice. I felt angry with myself for censoring my views. I had cancelled myself, for God's sake! How did this happen? I was a strong woman. I spoke up about all sorts of things all the time. Why was everything so different now? Where did my courage go? What was I so afraid of? How had the world shifted so rapidly into everything being measured by the left's virtuous presentation of what's moral and right with complete and utter intolerance for anything different? I chose to blow off some of the pressure inside of me with a bellowing message on International Women's Day in March 2021. My entire business up until that point was rooted in women's empowerment, yet I knew that if I were to bring all of these women into the same room they'd shred each other to bits if they held a different view. It felt like the very community I had created for women to use their voices and share their stories in, wouldn't allow the space and acceptance for me to do the same. How did this happen?

***

Isolation.

When I gave myself permission to speak, I knew I'd face backlash. I knew I'd lose business. I knew I'd lose relationships. Because I knew that shutting down dialogue that made others feel uncomfortable was simply what had been normalized and deemed the socially acceptable way to deal with disagreements. Nuance wasn't permissible. Anything that challenged a person's belief was a surefire way to be removed from social circles and gatherings, and anything that challenged what the talking heads on television were saying enraged people and filled them with animosity for reasons they couldn't even articulate other than #trustthescience. With the freedom to use my voice came the sacrifice of people in my life, as slowly they began to make their way out of my spaces. I was either blocked, unfollowed, shamed, muted, or asked to stop talking about it altogether if interactions were in person. Shocking headlines suggesting the unvaccinated should be left to die so we didn't take up any hospital beds with our selfishness, or at minimum, uninvited to Thanksgiving dinner, became the norm in the media. I had never experienced anything so maddening. So defeating. So isolating. It felt like one of those nightmares where you try to scream to warn others about imminent danger, only no sound comes out, and there was no waking up from it.

* * *

I need help.

I told my husband I was going to find a therapist one evening in the fall of 2021 through swollen, tearful, and exhausted eyes. I had spent months trying to get anyone to hear my concerns. It didn't matter what facts or concrete science I shared – I had a Google doc a mile long by that point. It never mattered what glaringly obvious, nefarious dialogue and behaviours happening in our government I pointed out. It was clear that I held little power over the television screens that had captivated the masses. To boot, I was no longer allowed on planes. I wasn't allowed to dine in restaurants or take part in most extra-curricular activities. Most of the people in my life had quietly vanished. I couldn't remember the last time I had been invited anywhere. In a matter of months, we had gone from vaccines and free ice cream cones to "take this vaccine or you'll lose your job and access to most people and things you love." To make matters worse, our Prime Minister had been freshly re-elected after a gruelling and divisive campaign against people like me. It was no longer the government I feared the most – it was the people who supported them that terrified me. How on earth any human with a beating heart could get behind medical segregation for a virus with a near ninety-nine percent survival rate, and a vaccine that did not stop transmission or prevent infection was beyond me. How anyone could swallow their food in a restaurant while others weren't allowed to even enter because of their own private medical decision spoke volumes to me, for just how easy it was for our government to manipulate people so deeply that they were willing to leave their friends and family behind in order to enjoy life's simple pleasures. The pain was unrelenting. I, the visionary, the big dreamer, the future planner, suddenly couldn't see past the end of each day. The darkness that had enveloped our world felt thick enough to cut with a knife, yet so many couldn't even see it. Blinded by the promise of a moral badge of honour and their freedoms being restored in exchange for their compliance. Freedoms they so easily gave up in exchange for a false sense of security. It was as if I was the only sober one in a world full of drunks. I could see the problem so clearly, but to everyone else, it seemed to go unnoticed. I was out of tools from my personal development toolbox. It was time to bring in a pro.

Hope

With immense fortune, I found a therapist I could trust with my experiences, thoughts, and views. So many people I knew were facing so much shame cast upon them by the very people there to support their mental welfare, which made it difficult to trust who I opened up to. I told her that all I felt was anger. Anger that was so visceral it scared me. When we started working together, I shared that by 7:00 am each morning, I was at my breaking point and for the remainder of each day, the rage would rattle around inside my body with nowhere to go, and I was afraid of how it would manifest itself in my physical health. It wasn't just because I was being punished for choosing not to get vaccinated. It was the pain of not being heard or seen. It was the pain of no one understanding what I was trying to tell them, and their apathetic responses. It was too much to bear. I challenged their worldviews too deeply. The constant rejection, dismissal, and isolation that drove me to prioritize my mental health are also what pushed me to leave my home at 3:45 am on a cold January morning in an act of hope that a bunch of truckers might be able to stop the madness from penetrating our lives any further.

As my therapy continued, I allowed myself to keep unravelling my pain and working through it. As I dedicated my time to healing and strengthening myself, my voice continued to grow louder, my confidence grew stronger, and my conviction in the truth, deepened. I never did make it to Ottawa. By the time I got to Medicine Hat, Alberta, with the convoy, I had seen what I needed to see. I wasn't alone! And there was no hiding this! In fact, there were so many people lined up on overpasses and standing shoulder to shoulder on the sides of the road waving signs and flags with tears pouring from their eyes, it changed me for the better on a cellular level. I felt safe again in my own country. People of all ages, cultures, and walks of life. Together. United in love, freedom, and truth. I had hope.

The Great Paradox

During a call with my therapist post-convoy, I expressed a bizarre situation I was experiencing. On one hand, I felt completely robbed of my freedoms and my future. There had never been more restriction, control, and red tape around my very existence here on earth. And I had never experienced so much loss. While on the other hand, I had never felt stronger and more liberated. I was speaking freely, with confidence, and without fear. I had regained control of my own life in a way that felt beautifully authentic. I felt excited about my own future again. And the amazing people I had wondered about my whole life, were suddenly before me. How could these two experiences be happening simultaneously?

My therapist replied with, "You had to lose your freedoms, to find your freedom."

The great paradox. In that moment, as I heard my therapist

communicate back to me what she was hearing in my dialogue, my entire journey became worth it. Without it, I wouldn't have found the real me that had been so deeply buried beneath layers of conditioning. Conditioning and social expectations I once believed I had cleared from my path, only to rediscover just how present it all still was when my feet were held to the flames. Personal sovereignty is not something our government grants us. It's something we are born with. The further we drift away from ourselves and our inner knowing is what paves the way for group think, collectivism, and damaging levels of government control under the illusion of morality. It is our duty to be sovereign individuals, so collectively we can be the best we can be.

To me, sovereignty *is* the great paradox.

Love and loss.
Acceptance and rejection.
Unity and division.
Growth and pain.
Reward and punishment.
Support and challenge
Ease and friction.

It's our fear of loss, rejection, division, pain, punishment, challenge, and friction that prevent us from leaning into our sovereignty, even though it's precisely how we access the fullest experience of love, acceptance, unity, growth, reward, support, and ease in our lives. The journey to personal freedom, if you commit to it, is worth it every time. Don't let them tell you otherwise.

SARAH SWAIN

Sarah is a high-energy entrepreneur and business strategist that quit her job in 2017, with no backup plan and trusted herself to fly. She has taken the Canadian entrepreneurial scene by storm as she is passionate about helping people reinstate the power of choice in their lives, by creating more wealth and independence. Sarah, like many of us, has navigated the unpredictable terrain of the past two years both as a professional and as an everyday Canadian, becoming a major voice for freedom fighters across the nation - a journey that has stripped her of any remaining shred of inauthenticity. With a knack for Canadian politics, Sarah has also become a source of simplifying our Parliamentary proceedings and played a significant role in helping people build the confidence needed to enact change as citizens of a democracy. Sarah resides in the foothills of the Alberta Rockies with her family, in the cabin in the woods she swore she'd always move to.

To my husband Rob, my therapist Sarah, and the incredible people who have shown up in this beautiful community. Thank you.

Never Stop
trusting yourself!

(signature)

A Sovereign Prayer

May you always know your power.
May you always live fully.
May you always lead with love.
May you always be curious.
May you always allow yourself to experience joy.
May you always bless yourself with laughter.
May you always show up in your light.
May you always know your truth.
May you always allow yourself to grow.
May you always blaze trails for those behind you.
May you always see what's possible for you.
May you always stand for what's right.
May you always live with inner peace.
May you always have the strength you need.
May you always trust your inner compass.
May you always feel the power of unity.
May you always seek and provide solutions.
May you always know your heart.
May you always lead with integrity.
May you always seek the truth.
May you always know your freedom.
May these stories be forever told.

REFERENCES

Chapter 1

Elizabeth Gilbert, *Eat, Pray, Love* (Penguin Publishing, February 16, 2006)

Snoop Dogg, Walk of Fame Speech, Hollywood California, November, 2018

Chapter 2

Dr. Kelly Brogan https://kellybroganmd.mykajabi.com/ blog?page=4&tag=hormones

Maya Angelou, Quoted in *"No surrender"* by Gary Younge, www.theguardian.com. May 24, 2002.

Chapter 4

C.S. Lewis, *The Screwtape Letters* (United Kingdon, Geoffrey Bles, 1942)

Public Health and Medical Professionals for Transparency, https://phmpt.org/

World health Organization Vigi Access, https://www.vigiaccess.org/

Center of Disease Control and Prevention (CDC) Vaccine Adverse Event Reporting System, (VAERS) https://vaers.hhs.gov/

Government of Canada, https://health-infobase.canada.ca/covid-19/vaccine-safety/summary.html

Chapter 5

College of Physicians and Surgeons of Ontario (CPSO) https://www.cpso.on.ca/

Center of Disease Control and Prevention (CDC), https://www.cdc.gov/coronavirus/2019-ncov/index.html

Jenna Greene (2022, Jan 7) 'Paramount importance': Judge orders FDA to hasten release of Pfizer vaccine docs https://www.reuters.com/legal/government/paramount-importance-judge-orders-fda-hasten-release-pfizer-vaccine-docs-2022-01-07/

Norman Doidge (2022, Jan 22) Vaccines are a tool, not a silver bullet. If we'd allowed more scientific debate, we would have realized this earlier https://www.theglobeandmail.com/opinion/article-vaccines-are-a-tool-not-a-silver-bullet-if-wed-allowed-more-scientific/

Chapter 7

Peter Crone, coach-The Mind Architect, b.1971 https://www.petercrone.com/

Dr. Wayne W. Dyer-*Feeling Good Is Feeling God* podcast air date December 16, 2018

Snoop Dogg, Walk of Fame Speech, Hollywood California, November, 2018

Chapter 8

Elections Canada

https://www.elections.ca/content.aspx?section=res&dir=rep/off/cou&document=index44&lang=e

Chapter 12

I Believe That We Will Win (World Anthem) by Pitbull, released 2020

Chapter 13

Margaret Mead, quoted in: Kabir, Hajara Muhammad (2010). Northern women development. [Nigeria]. ISBN 978-978-906-469-4. OCLC 890820657

Chapter 14

Nadine Yousif, (2021, Aug 26) 'When it comes to empathy for the unvaccinated, many of us aren't feeling it'
https://www.thestar.com/news/gta/2021/08/26/when-it-comes-to-empathy-for-the-unvaccinated-many-of-us-arent-feeling-it.html?li_source=LI&li_medium=star_web_ymbii

Chapter 15

Vaccine Adverse Event Reporting System (VAERS) https://vaers.hhs.gov/
Center for Disease Control and Prevention (CDC), https://www.cdc.gov/coronavirus/2019-ncov/index.html
World Health Organization Vigi Access, https://www.vigiaccess.org/

Government of Canada, https://health-infobase.canada.ca/covid-19/
vaccine-safety/summary.html

Jeff Eikenburg

Chelsie Meyer

Ashley Correia

Thank you for supporting us.
Thank you for hearing us.
Thank you for seeing us.

Lisa Musso

Sarah Morrison

Rosanna Di Fiore

Rebecca Floris